The Characteristics of Effective Learning

The characteristics of effective learning – playing and exploring, active learning and creating and thinking critically – underpin young children's learning and development and are central to the revised Early Years Foundation Stage. Practitioners need to be confident of planning, observing and assessing characteristics of effective learners and understand how they support children's learning and development.

The book explores what the characteristics of effective learning look like and how practitioners can create opportunities for children to express them. It considers the ways in which they connect with children's natural explorations, play, enjoyment and the environments created by adults. Throughout the book, the focus is on building on children's own interests as practitioners plan for, observe and assess playing and exploring, active learning and creativity and critical thinking.

Including encounters from authentic settings and provocative questions for reflective practice, the book covers:

- children's well-being and motivations
- creating effective learning possibilities for all children
- engaging children's interests
- the role of the adult and environment
- sustained shared thinking.

This timely new text aims to help practitioners and students develop their understanding of the characteristics of effective learning and show them how they can support young children in becoming effective and motivated learners.

Annie Woods is Senior Lecturer in Early Years at Nottingham Trent University, UK.

The Characteristics of Effective Learning

Creating and capturing the possibilities in the early years

Edited by Annie Woods

Routledge
Taylor & Francis Group

LONDON AND NEW YORK

First published 2015
by Routledge
2 Park Square, Milton Park, Abingdon, Oxon OX14 4RN

Simultaneously published in the USA and Canada
by Routledge
711 Third Avenue, New York, NY 10017

Routledge is an imprint of the Taylor & Francis Group, an informa business

British Library Cataloguing in Publication Data
A catalogue record for this book is available from the British Library

Library of Congress Cataloging in Publication Data
The characteristics of effective learning: creating and capturing the
     possibilities in the early years/edited by Annie Woods.
     pages cm
     Includes bibliographical references.
     Summary 1. Learning. 2. Early childhood education. I. Woods,
     Annie.
     LB1060.C4685 2014
     372.21 – dc23
     2014012512

ISBN: 978-0-415-73792-0 (hbk)
ISBN: 978-0-415-73793-7 (pbk)
ISBN: 978-1-315-75263-1 (ebk)

Typeset in Palatino
by Florence Production Ltd, Stoodleigh, Devon, UK

MIX
Paper from
responsible sources
FSC
www.fsc.org   FSC® C013604

Printed and bound by CPI Group (UK) Ltd, Croydon, CR0 4YY

Contents

Contributors

Victoria Brown has been a primary and early years teacher in schools in Nottingham and Nottinghamshire for 17 years. She has also worked as a local authority foundation stage advisory teacher and mentor for private, voluntary or independent (PVI) settings and led practice in a children's centre. She moved to Nottingham Trent University in 2006, where she works as a senior lecturer and programme leader in primary and early years initial teacher education.

Catherine Gripton was a teacher for 14 years in Nottingham and Nottinghamshire primary schools, teaching children across the 3–7 age range and becoming an advanced skills teacher in 2003. She is a senior lecturer in primary and early years initial teacher education at Nottingham Trent University.

Val Hall has worked as a senior lecturer in childhood studies at Nottingham Trent University. She has extensive experience as a special education teacher and senior manager within mainstream and generic special schools and as a local authority advisory teacher for autism and behaviour.

Vicky McEwan has worked in a variety of early years roles. She started her working life as a nursery nurse, before training to become a teacher. Vicky owned and managed her own day nursery for many years, before moving into early years advisory work, supporting schools and settings to provide high-quality experiences for young children and their families. Vicky then spent a number of years lecturing on early years programmes at Nottingham Trent University. Vicky is a trained forest school leader and has run forest school programmes alongside a children's centre for children and their families. She currently works as a school improvement officer for early years, working across the sector. Vicky has two young daughters who keep her grounded in the reality of young children's needs.

Moira Moran taught and led teams in nursery units and schools for more than 20 years, first in London then in Nottingham. She subsequently joined a team of local authority early years specialist teachers supporting the PVI sector and teachers in foundation units. She has been involved with the Early Years Professional Status from its inception, as lecturer, mentor and assessor. Now at Nottingham Trent

University, she leads the childhood studies course, in addition to lecturing on the early years strand of primary teacher education. Her research area is early play, and she has recently become a forest school trainer.

Sharon Vesty is Senior Lecturer in Childhood Studies at Nottingham Trent University's School of Education. She is a psychotherapist (UKCP registered) and a registered general nurse. Sharon has extensive experience of health care practice and management and counselling and psychotherapy with young people and adults, having worked both in the NHS and private practice. Sharon has a special interest in self-esteem and well-being issues in children and young people.

Lorna Wardle has a wealth of experience as an early years practitioner in schools and has been a manager, trainer and local authority advisor. This involved offering advice, support, guidance, challenge and training to early years providers in the non-maintained sector. She now works at Nottingham Trent University as an early years lecturer, with responsibility for the delivery and development of the early years strand and programme leadership of Joint Honours in Education. In addition, she has also delivered teaching on the childhood studies course, MA Early Years and BA (Hons) Education.

Annie Woods is an experienced early years lecturer at Nottingham Trent University. Previously responsible for programme development for childhood studies, the early years specialist route for teaching and early years subject development for the Joint Honours programme in Education, she now has a particular interest in outdoor play environments and children's fascination with natural elements, and she works part-time helping to lead learning in nature modules. She is a trained forest school leader.

Acknowledgements

For these little, and some grown up people, we would like to say that without you affording us the opportunity to watch, listen, learn and love, our ideas and thoughts may not have come to fruition: thank you to Freya and Eden, Tilly and Charlie, Marc, Amy and Alba, Dorrie and Bill, Patrick, Simon and Tim, Susie, Lois and Vanessa, Ed, Tom and Emma, Brendan and Aidan, Max and Gabriel, and the encountered children who grace this book with their capabilities, imagination and wonder.

Introduction

Annie Woods

This book is written with an optimistic tone, to support practitioners in asserting their practice of observing, planning, celebrating and enjoying children's learning dispositions, particularly at a time when effective early years practice faces what we see as one of its greatest challenges. The authors use established theoretical principles to restate how and what effective practice can look like, and where environment and practitioner resourcefulness are attuned to the unique characteristics of effective learning of children in a variety of settings and contexts. In this way, we also intend to develop students' and newly qualified practitioners' professional and philosophical ideas and practice.

Each chapter is written from experience. The authors are keen observers of both children and practitioners, having developed expertise themselves and regularly monitor and support students and developing practitioners in a diverse range of settings. We use the term encounters to examine what we *perceive* may be happening for a child or child and adult, aware that our subjectivity is one of the ways we can further reflect on both our own and the participants' experience. As 'watchers' or co-participants, the encounters always present fleeting and fluid insights and are always the start of the next process, rather than the end picture. These authentic encounters are discussed interpretively, or, as Dahlberg (1999, in Dahlberg and Moss, 2005: 107) argues, as 'a process of making practice visible'. The encounters have involved us in reflection, and, during the process of selection of observations we have both seen and taken part in, we have been:

> open to the 'possibles' (possible interpretations, multiple dialogues among children and adults) [as part of a process]: while each fragment is imbued with the subjectivity of the documenter, it is offered to the interpretative subjectivity of others in order to be known or re-known, created or recreated. The reader can be a colleague, a group of colleagues, a child, children, [and] parents, anyone who has participated or wants to participate in this process. The documentation material is open, accessible, usable, and therefore readable.
> (Rinaldi, 2001a, 2001b, in Dahlberg and Moss, 2005: 108)

The chapters, opening with encounters and ending with provocations, reflect our understanding of Reggio Emilia and closely follow our first book, *Child-Initiated Play and Learning: Planning for Possibilities in the Early Years* (2013), written by the same authors, who both practise as teachers or advisors and teach early years and childhood studies students, having shared many of the presented encounters as case studies for discussion. Our aim is for you to think about what you see, and observe a child, not from only one perspective or the linear tree model of development, but from multiple viewpoints, rather like digging down to find the iris flower bulb and finding all the bulb shoots that are emerging sideways. It is also like peeling away at the layers of an onion: a child's play and schematic interests are likely to have more layers and effective learning activity than a single response to our invented work tasks. Characteristics of effective learning are in these layers. This is rhizoanalysis – thinking about an idea, a problem, an observation, a child's project or idea, not as a logical journey to a specific outcome, but an odd, unique and distinctive reaction or suggestion as to *how* they set about a task or establish their play or build relationships: *what is on and below the surface*.

For us, this 'iceberg' is a means of looking at and documenting children's characteristics of effective learning, as enshrined in the revised Early Years Foundation Stage (EYFS) Statutory Framework (Department for Education, 2012: 1.10), where it states:

> In planning and guiding children's activities, practitioners must reflect on the different ways that children learn and reflect these in their practice.
> The three characteristics of effective teaching and learning are:
>
> ■ playing and exploring – children investigate and experience things, and 'have a go';
>
> ■ active learning – children concentrate and keep on trying if they encounter difficulties, and enjoy achievements; and
>
> ■ creating and thinking critically – children have and develop their own ideas, make links between ideas, and develop strategies for doing things.

These are further expanded in the non-mandatory guidance *Development Matters in the Early Years Foundation Stage (EYFS)* (Early Education, 2012).

This non-mandatory guidance is no longer provided to practitioners, and the brevity of the current statutory guidelines, alongside new profile and assessment guidelines for our youngest children, implies that the characteristics are no longer valued as important indicators of a child's unique achievements. We would argue, however, that long-established early years pedagogy is underpinned by a tradition of looking carefully at the process of *how* children learn, because this will amplify *what* they have learned, and, in a series of chapters, the authors carefully unpick a continuum of practice, observation, learning and interpretation and the universality of *effective teaching*, as well as effective learning, despite a continued, dynamic culture of changing political and interventionist strategies.

Characteristics of effective learning are underpinned by the ideas of Montessori, Isaacs, Piaget, Vygotsky, Bruner, Katz, Laevers and Malaguzzi; they form the basis of the approach of Reggio Emilia, the curriculum of New Zealand and outstanding practice within the UK. We would argue that they can be seen in children's increasing ability, through confidence and experience, to 'tap into' a reservoir of assimilated 'know-how' and succeed, without giving up, floundering or necessarily asking for support when faced with a 'hiccup' or momentary new problem. If support is required, however, it can be seen to be assuredly sought, acknowledged, used/adapted and added to a working, effective repertoire of actions. Essentially, these characteristics are successful learning dispositions.

In order to develop, absorb and present characteristics of effective learning, children need to be exposed to rich opportunities:

> the curricular food that will nourish and strengthen children's powers; their (the educators') second responsibility is to organise children's enquiries and experiences so that they are actively and emotionally engaged, exploring those aspects of the world that really matter to them, for themselves, with their own hands and eyes and voices, with their own observations, theories, experiments, discoveries and critical questions. And thirdly, through the regular practice of systematic observation, educators learn to value the learning they see going on before their eyes.
>
> (Rich *et al.*, 2005: 11)

Children should be supported to develop resourcefulness through active experiences and exposure to language, in order that they can express their ideas and creativity. It follows, then, that we have a duty to provide this exposure and *be prepared* to recognise, assess and celebrate powerful dispositions of independent thought and action, autonomy and positive wilfulness.

Early years practitioners have a strong identity; we have to be assertive and assured advocates for children who, from their earliest development, are learning how to learn. Through philosophical tradition, we are a community of learners who debate, challenge, question, enable, watch and play.

> Wenger (1998) suggests that learning is a characteristic of practice and that communities can be a site both for the *acquisition* of knowledge and for the *creation* of knowledge as a result of fine-tuning between participants' experiences and their competencies.
>
> (Cherrington and Thornton, 2013: 126)

The following chapters seek to help us enable and capture the skills, competencies and characteristics of very young children, as they are transformed into impressive human capacities (Rogoff, 1990).

In Chapter 1, Vicky McEwan warmly embraces the reader in thinking about pre- and post-birth playful exchanges that set the scene for complex cognitive development. The delightful encounters are analysed carefully and are a useful guide for practitioners who are puzzling over documenting babies' characteristics of effective learning. The encounter of an unborn baby resonated with Catherine, who recounted her own experience of carrying twin girls: they could be seen playing with each other and mirroring each other's movements while being scanned *in utero*. As children, they can still be observed in close sleeping and playing positions, emotionally and physically attached, playing with language and ideas as they effectively face challenges and new experiences together. Freya's encounter can also be compared to Kieran's encounter in Chapter 4, where first-hand experience is stored (assimilated) and becomes relevant to subsequent action, essential to effective learning. What is emphasised here is the need to watch children's interactions with people, places and things, to see peer teaching and effective strategies that are copied, or social play where children are demonstrating their cultural and familial experiences. Vicky's provocation demands that we are mindful of children's patterns of development, shaped by the unique dispositions and contextual experiences of their early years.

The encounters considered in Chapter 1 give an illustration of children who exhibit high levels of well-being and involvement in a range of experiential contexts. Lorna Wardle and Sharon Vesty further examine the connection between high levels of well-being and involvement and characteristics of effective learning, through practical and thoughtful encounters in Chapter 2. There are many settings that now use Laevers' (1994, 2002) scales to monitor both environment and the child/children within the environment, to ensure that a child is able to learn effectively and holistically across all developmental domains. Vicky's consideration of our role of knowing our parents and carers is extended as we are urged to know our children fully. Every practitioner is accountable here, underpinned by the manager/leader role in organising a happy, caring and trusting ethos in which children can 'fly', and parents are welcomed, valued, involved and seen as experts. We can see from the *everyday* encounters that characteristics of effective learning can be seen in a simple choosing activity, through body language and through attachments and, when documented, they give a full and detailed picture of every child's readiness, willingness and ability to show us what they can do and what they may be thinking about.

Knowing *how* children learn can help us to build on our understanding of *what* they should learn. As we have already noted, nurturing relationships help children to learn best, developing their resilience and engendering a sense of persistence when faced with difficulties. In Chapter 3, Val Hall emphasises how assessing characteristics of effective learning, where there is a clear focus on process rather than merely outcome, is more likely to be successful and, by definition, inclusive. This philosophy is especially true for children with additional needs; their journey may be slower, distinctive and, yes, even special, but the process is most definitely important and relies on key adults who are able to adopt a positive perspective and look for things a child 'can do'. Val explores how unique learning cultures can be personalised for all children and challenge any preconceptions, views and judgements that we may bring to our assessment of children. She cautions against labelling and underlines the importance of the key and effective learning characteristics of adults as crucial to a fully inclusive environment.

Annie Woods' first chapter, Chapter 4, considers the playfulness of children's learning and the *disposition* to be ready, willing and able to pursue a project or schema of ideas actively. It is in playfulness that we see characteristics of effective learning, children using what they know in their play and achieving what they set out to do, acquiring information through active exploration initiated by themselves, and then transforming resources though manipulation, connection and imagination. For practitioners, the challenge is providing the balance and blend of activities and opportunities for individual and group activity, child-led and adult-directed activity, when it appears clear that characteristics of effective learning are more easily observed during experiential and exploratory play, suggestive of more child-led enquiry.

Effective practitioners will encourage parents to share their children's engaging interests so that they can be built upon, as illustrated by Val in Chapter 3. In our settings, these longer-term projects or inquiries can be less noticeable, because of competing interests, pressures of external demands on our own and the children's time, and because of frequent changes in adult personnel, but the encounters included in this chapter give a real sense of optimism about the incredible capabilities of children that, given time and opportunity, we can document and interpret.

In Chapter 5, Catherine Gripton explains complex ideas with ease, bridging Annie's Chapters 4 and 6, where elements of children's explorations and longer-term projects and then the guided participation of adults are examined. It is complementary to Victoria Brown's Chapter 7, where the importance of sustained conversations is discussed. Attention to children's thinking during observation of child-initiated activity reveals much about their learning and supports practitioners in gaining a deep knowledge of the child. This builds a complex and distinct picture, where patterns, preferences – often subconscious – and approaches appear. In reporting upon creative and critical thinking when documenting learning, Catherine gives us information on our interpretation of how each unique child learns, and this is explored further in the final chapter of the book. Attention to thinking in assessment does more than prompt us to include how a child learns; it urges us to consider how our provision provides the landscape for thinking.

The focus of Chapter 6 is to consider how guided participation is the enhanced role good and effective practitioners can play when they work alongside children and support their characteristics of effective learning. Annie examines the ideas of Rogoff extensively and the extent to which apprenticeship of children to more experienced others is the means by which children demonstrate actual, proximal and future development, and cultural transformation occurs. All encounters involve the author as participant or documenter, which adds authenticity to the interpretation and analysis. They demonstrate that adjusted support, which takes into account each child's willingness and ability to participate using a range of skills and attributes, to avoid unnecessary and devaluing interventions and enhancements, and which is both challenging and sensitive to the developing curiosity and resilience of children, underpins the creation of possibilities for children to develop the many active characteristics of effective learning.

Victoria continues to elaborate on the sustained conversations children have with adults and each other in Chapter 7, which builds on key ideas introduced in Chapter 1, where Vicky demonstrates, through her descriptions of early encounters between adults and babies, how human beings are pre-programmed to interact and share experiences with those who are familiar to them. This chapter takes two key principles that can be seen to underpin effective communication encounters and suggests how adults can create a positive emotional and physical environment, where thinking is stimulated, sustained and shared with others through reciprocal interaction and conversation. This chapter, therefore, strives to deepen practitioners' understanding of the value of engaging in sustained shared thinking with children at different developmental stages and focuses on the role of *sustained shared interaction and conversation* as a key tool or context in nurturing and supporting this with children.

Through offering informal and more structured encounters with children at home and in a range of settings, this chapter considers children's different communication preferences, verbal and non-verbal. It argues that sustained shared thinking and interaction can occur in everyday moments, wherever and whenever adults are engaged with children, and whether these moments are initiated by adults or by children or occur in informal or more formal contexts.

In the final chapter, Moira Moran helps us to understand the 'capturing' of evidence of characteristics of effective learning. All the authors have, to some extent and through encounters, demonstrated this and, in addition, shown how to afford opportunities and possibilities for creating rich learning environments. Moira states that it is important to consider that, although observation and assessment are the subject of this final chapter, they are by no means the last things to think about or do; rather they permeate everything we think about and do with the children in our care so that we can best provide for them. Observing the characteristics of children's learning can require a new lens through which to observe *how* children learn, rather than *what* they learn, to look at what we are seeing, rather than to see what we are looking for.

Our intention, then, is to provoke reflection and questions, not to provide a template or the answers; Sonnyboy in Chapter 4 would have something to say about that! The aim is the same for you, the readers, as it would be for the children we enjoy learning with. Deleuze and Parnet (1989: 9, in Dahlberg and Moss, 2005: 107) offer you this final thought and image:

> If you are not allowed to invent your questions from all over the place, from never mind where, if people pour them into you, you haven't much to say. While encountering others, and while each child is bringing in her/his lot, a becoming is sketched out between the different perspectives. Then a block starts moving, a block which no longer belongs to anyone, but is 'between' everyone . . . Like a little boat which children let slip and loose, and is stolen by others.

References

Cherrington, S. and Thornton, K. (2013) Continuing professional development in early childhood education in New Zealand. *Early Years: An International Research Journal* 33(2): 119–32.

Dahlberg, G. and Moss, P. (2005) *Ethics and Politics in Early Childhood Education*. London: RoutledgeFalmer.

Department for Education (2012) *Statutory Framework for the Early Years Foundation Stage (EYFS)*. Cheshire, UK: Department for Education.

Early Education (2012) *Development Matters in the Early Years Foundation Stage (EYFS)*. London: Early Education.

Laevers, F. (ed.) (1994) *The Leuven Involvement Scale for Young Children*. LIS-YC Manual. Leuven, Belgium: Centre for Experiential Education.

Laevers, F. (2002) *Research on Experiential Education Reader: A Selection of Articles by Ferre Laevers*. Leuven, Belgium: Centre for Experiential Education.

Rich, D., Casanova, D., Dixon, A., Drummond, M.J., Durrant, A. and Myer, C. (2005) *First Hand Experience: What Matters to Children*. Clopton, UK: Rich Learning Opportunities.

Rogoff, B. (1990) *Apprenticeship in Thinking: Cognitive Development in Social Context*. Oxford, UK: Oxford University Press.

Woods, A. (ed.) (2013) *Child-Initiated Play and Learning: Planning for Possibilities in the Early Years*. London: Routledge.

1

Children are naturally playful

Vicky McEwan

In this chapter, we will explore child development through children's everyday play encounters with people, places and things, and begin to consider play in the womb and continue using encounters of children as they grow and develop. Although this book is not intended as a child development text, it is essential we read the following chapters with an understanding of children's development, using a range of key theories and scientific understanding of the development of the body and the brain as a lens through which to understand children's playful learning and the characteristics of effective learning.

Pre-natal play

Forbes (2004) suggests that babies begin to play in the womb, and scans of the foetus show how early babies appear to play. The encounter below supports Forbes' thinking.

Encounter: the 20-week scan

An expectant mother is being scanned at 20 weeks. As the image comes to life on screen, the baby is seen to extend her arms above her head and then move down as if on a slide; this action is repeated several times, and the baby appears to be playing, stretching her arms and legs before sliding down to bended knees and arms at the sides.

This encounter demonstrates the playful nature of foetuses as they explore their body and movement in their environment, the womb. Children are observed to be naturally playful from birth; from only moments old, a young baby will look at and focus on the mother's face and will make attempts to copy her facial movements (Murray and Andrews, 2000). These early encounters with people demonstrate how the human species is pre-programmed to interact in order to both survive and to develop; the second encounter highlights these amazing capabilities from a newborn baby.

Encounter: the new arrival

In a busy labour ward, a new baby has just been born. She lies cradled in her mother's arms, next to her mother's skin; the baby turns her head towards her mother and begins to root, searching for her first feed; she finds the nipple and grasps it, sucking hard. After a few moments of sucking, she releases and looks up towards her mother's face; she looks intently as her mother speaks to the midwife and then, as the conversation ends and her mother falls silent, she turns her face towards the breast and begins to root again.

This early encounter in the first few moments of life shows us some of the very early learning that has already taken place in the womb. The rooting reflex is essential for survival: babies need to latch on to be fed, and the baby has been practising this skill in the womb. At around 25 weeks, in the womb, a baby's hand co-ordination allows them to bring their hand to their face; at this stage, the face and lips are an area of high sensitivity and provide the baby with an early sensory experience (Blott, 2009). The mouth continues to be the tool the baby uses to explore for many months to come, both inside and outside the womb. In the human foetus:

> The first region . . . [to develop] is the part that will represent the mouth and tongue in the motor and sematosensory areas of the brain. The cortex then goes on to develop in concentric zones outward from this core region.
>
> (Goddard Blythe, 2005: 51)

We can see that this early rooting is not only associated with the primitive need for food for survival, but is a key tool in a baby's explorations of the world, both inside and outside the womb.

This encounter also shows us how a newborn baby is able to tune in to sounds that are familiar, as the baby stopped sucking to look at her mother who was speaking. The baby has heard her mother's voice for many months in the womb, and it is a very familiar sound to her. The human foetus can hear from about 24–26 weeks, as the fluid that surrounds the baby in the womb allows sound to pass to the baby from the outside world, although the sounds they hear may be slightly different, because of the fluid and tissue that have surrounded them. The fluid and tissue only allow lower frequencies to be passed through, and, therefore, babies are unable to hear higher-pitched sounds. Although not all sounds are fully heard, babies in the womb still respond to sound, and mothers often report that the baby will move suddenly in response to a loud noise; ultrasound scans also show the foetus will give a 'blink-startle' response to a sudden loud noise (Blott, 2009). Research has also shown how babies as young as 4 days old respond to the language spoken by their mother, which has surrounded them in the womb, above other languages. Karmiloff and Karmiloff-Smith (2001) cite a study by French researchers who found that babies sucked harder when hearing French voices over Russian voices, but that there was no change in their sucking pattern or rate when they heard Russian and then English voices.

Early language

If we look at the second encounter, we can see many of the characteristics of effective early learning being displayed when the baby is only moments old. This baby was showing an interest in people, in this instance her mother, as she stopped sucking and turned to listen; she also used her senses to explore as she rooted; both of these are key elements of playing and exploring.

This next encounter also focuses on hearing, along with the connection between hearing and production of sound.

Encounter: Twinkle, twinkle . . . all join in!

At bedtime, two siblings are settling down for sleep; one is aged 3, the other only 4 months. The 3-year-old is in bed and requests the mother to sing a well-known song; the mother is feeding the 4-month-old in a chair by the bed. The mother begins to sing 'Twinkle, twinkle', and the 3-year-old joins in with her; after the first few lines, the baby stops sucking and drops away from the breast; she listens and then begins to make vocal sounds, as if joining in with the familiar song. The sounds the baby makes are like a little melody and vary in pitch. Once the singing is finished, after 'Twinkle, twinkle' has been sung through three times, the baby stops her melody of cooing sounds and returns to feed. The older child comments, 'Oh that was good, we all joined in, she can sing now, soon she will be able to talk too.'

From birth, babies communicate by crying, making eye contact and bodily movements; for example, a baby who is very distressed will not only cry but will kick their legs and wave their arms, to show just how cross and distressed they are, whereas a baby who wants to be picked up will cry and look towards the caregiver, trying to catch her attention. Carers of young babies are able to recognise the different cries their baby makes and what they are trying to communicate through their cry. Babies will coo (produce a sound) at about 3 months and babble (repeating the same sounds) at about 6 months. Chomsky (1965) suggested that children are born with a language acquisition device, meaning we are pre-wired to learn language patterns and grammar; however, Bruner (1983) believed that language is developed as a consequence of the social and emotional relationships we have with those closest to us, our main caregivers and siblings.

This encounter links together hearing and the production of sound, as the baby responded verbally to what she heard. Her communication of sound was meaningful: she was clearly joining in with the singing, a song she had heard many times, previously as a member of the audience, but this time she was a participant. This was acknowledged by the older child as she commented on her sister's sound production as joining in and the precursor to talking. The use of the voice for sound production during children's play and encounters is essential in developing orientation of sound, attention, sound discrimination and memory (Goddard Blyth, 2005), but it is also about the need to communicate, to develop a voice, to be part of a group and to share encounters. Murray and Andrews (2000) demonstrate how young babies soon show a preference for the people who are connected and familiar to them, and that they do not just want to spend time with them and be physically close, but they want to interact and share experiences.

This encounter illustrates the coming together of all this theoretical understanding: developmentally, the baby was cooing and moving into babbling, and she chose to demonstrate this new-found voice by interacting with those to whom she is emotionally connected at a time of day when everyone was calm and relaxed and there were no external distractions.

Heuristic play

Looking at the characteristics of effective learning, we can see many elements of playing and exploring here, in this third encounter. The young baby was involved in a new experience and showing an interest in the activity going on around her. We can also see elements of active learning, as she maintained her focus until the singing had stopped.

Encounter: playing with treasures

Thomas is a baby of 8 months old and he can sit unsupported. He is sitting with a treasure basket containing various objects, such as a shell, a metal whisk, wooden balls, keys, corks, wicker coaster, etc. His childminder sits close by, observing his play. Thomas picks up a few items and quickly discards them, putting them at the side of the basket; he then tries to pick up the shell, but it is too heavy; he looks towards his childminder, who smiles her encouragement, and he tries again, but it just rolls over. He then turns his attention to the metal whisk: he picks it up and brings it to his mouth, pulls it out, looks at it and then puts it back in his mouth. He drops it, and it makes a noise as it hits a metal dish he has already taken out of the basket; he smiles and picks up the whisk and bangs it on various items at random; he smiles when the whisk connects with an item that makes a noise. He then brings the whisk once again to his mouth, mouthing it while looking around. He then turns his attention to other objects and, as he picks out a wooden ball, it rolls away. He tracks it with his eyes and then looks towards his childminder and makes a grunt; she acknowledges his sound by saying, 'Oh did it roll away, didn't you want that to roll?' He then picks out the whisk once again and continues to explore it in his mouth and by turning it in his hands. After several more minutes' play, he starts to rub his eyes and make a whining sound. This signals that he has finished, and his childminder acknowledges this and picks him up.

We can relate this encounter to the second encounter in this chapter, as Thomas is using his mouth to explore, just as the baby does during rooting and feeding. As Thomas uses his mouth and other senses to explore the objects during his play, messages are sent to his brain. Young children's brains are unfinished at birth and are very malleable, and, therefore, it is essential they have rich learning and development opportunities in secure, safe relationships to allow the brain to reach its full potential. The messages that flood the brain from sensory activities allow cells to signal to one another, strengthening the neural pathways in the brain (Gopnik *et al.*, 1999). The more the pathways are used, the stronger they get. This process of connection between the cells is called a synapse; synapses are essential in wiring up or connecting the brain, and those connections that are not used will be pruned away. In this encounter, we can see the potential to support healthy brain development, through the baby's interaction with people – his childminder – and things – the objects in the basket. Thomas is clearly connected to his childminder: she acknowledges his cues and responds to him, and this relationship provides him with a safe place to explore his treasure basket. The materials in the basket provide Thomas with a variety of sensory explorations as he creates sound, turns objects to examine what they look and feel like and discovers properties such as heavy and light. Robinson (2008) cites a 2003 study by Nielsen that explains how a young baby, between 4 and 8 months, learns about the existence of objects through their early explorations, which provide them with sensory feedback. We have already discussed how babies in the womb obtain sensory feedback as they bring their hands to their face and lips; this sensory feedback continues to be a vital tool in children's learning about themselves and their world. The key here is repetition, as demonstrated by Thomas returning over and over again to the whisk; he explores it in a range of ways, mouthing it, moving it, looking at it and feeling it, giving him a sense of that object and how it differs from the other objects in his basket. He also begins to use it for a purpose, when he recognises it makes a sound and then repeats the banging action. Using objects for a purpose, Nielson (ibid.) suggests, emerges at between 6 and 15 months. Thomas, at 8 months, is just starting to understand this concept.

We also see Thomas tracking objects here, as the ball rolls away from him and he follows it with his eyes. Babies generally begin to track a moving object from about 3 months old; at 8 months, Thomas has the ability to see objects that are further away, allowing him to track the ball as it rolls some distance. This becomes a great motivation for movement as he develops crawling to retrieve the ball.

Relationships with people, places and things

In the second and third encounters, we see how very young babies are interested in others and are capable of forming close relationships; in the second encounter, we clearly see how a baby of 4 months is able to participate in an activity and enjoy being together. In the third encounter, we see Thomas grunt to gain the attention of his caregiver, who in turn acknowledges and verbalises what has happened. Manning-Morton and Thorpe (2001) identify important aspects of the key person's relationship, which includes providing a safe base by being both physically and emotionally available, interacting with words and acknowledging babies' feelings. The relationship Thomas has allows him to feel secure enough to explore independently for a sustained amount of time, allowing him to reach high levels of involvement in his activity (Laevers, 1994), which in turn provides him with the opportunity to gain more sensory feedback from the objects in the basket that have captured his curiosity.

In considering the characteristics of effective learning, we can see elements of all three here. First, playing and exploring, finding out and exploring: Thomas is curious about the objects, he uses his senses to explore in an open-ended way and he shows interest for one object over the others. Second, active learning – being involved and concentrating: Thomas maintains his focus for a sustained period of time; he is fascinated and involved. Finally, creating and thinking critically – making links: Thomas notices that some things he bangs the whisk on make a noise, whereas others do not; his smiling tells us that he noted this.

Encounter: I can crawl!

At a children's centre, a young mother arrives at a stay and play session. She pops her young child on the floor with the others and goes to hang their coats up. As she turns away, the child rolls from his back to his front and pushes up into the crawling position; he then starts to crawl after her. Another parent comments on his new-found crawling skill, and the young mother starts to complain how he is so difficult now because he can get everywhere. During the play session, the child crawls over to various objects that interest him, falling back into the kneeling position to explore them. In previous weeks, he had played with the soft blocks, books and other toys his mother had given him, but, this week, he constantly crawls to activities he hasn't tried before, such as the oats in a builders tray, kneeling back and grabbing a fistful – he then opens his fist and watches them fall back into the tray making 'oh' and 'ah' noises; or the outdoor-area sandpit, where he crawls in, kneels, picks up sand and smiles as it runs through his fingers. His mother spends the session retrieving him from these play activities and returns him to the carpet and baby toys, but they no longer hold his attention, and, within a minute or two, he is crawling off to the sand or oats again.

This encounter highlights how the physical development of movement, in this case crawling, opens up new worlds and experiences for children. Children all learn to crawl at different times, and some children may never crawl; crawling is not just a physical skill, but of importance to the development of the brain. When we crawl, three very important senses integrate. Goddard Blyth (2005) tells us that the vestibular system (relating to sense of motion and position) is the first one of the sensory systems to mature and is already wired up in the womb; it is under constant stimulation before birth and remains so after birth. Proprioception is the sense of the inner self and awareness of the body and body parts, and the visual system is being able to look into the distance as well as down at the hands. Integrating these senses is important for balance and an awareness of space and depth. As a young child crawls using opposite arm to leg, it requires both the right and left hemispheres of the brain to work at the same time, thus increasing communication between the two sides of the brain, which leads to improved co-ordination in later life, needed for reading, writing and physical and mathe-matical development.

In order for a young child to crawl, the symmetrical tonic neck reflex (STNR) needs to become inhibited. The STNR is one of the second set of pre-programmed reflexes, emerging between 6 and 9 months, and it has the function of telling the upper body to do the opposite of the lower body. With the STNR functioning, when the head goes down, the arms bend and the legs try to straighten; however, if the head goes up, the arms straighten, the legs bend and the bottom sinks into the ankles; this makes it impossible for the baby to get up on to all fours, and so this reflex has to become inhibited for crawling to develop, normally between 9 and 12 months.

As we can see from the encounter above the development of crawling is not only positive in terms of physical mobility and future learning, but the independ-ence associated with being able to move independently provides the child with new places to explore and the ability to make decisions about where they want to go and what they want to do, providing more opportunities to play and explore actively. This independence will in turn raise a child's self esteem and confidence providing they have a supportive carer to encourage their new found independence. As in the above encounter many parents find this transition from a non-mobile baby to a crawling baby very difficult and the use of equipment such as play pens, baby walkers and seats while essential in keeping babies safe at some points in the day should be limited to allow children the opportunity to benefit most from the crawling stage.

Engaging new experiences

The child in the fifth encounter demonstrates many of the characteristics of effective learning:

- playing and exploring – finding out and exploring: showing curiosity, using the senses and showing interest as he engaged with oats and sand; and
- playing and exploring – being willing to have a go: initiating activities and engaging in new experiences as he sought out the tactile play opportunities.

Encounter: an Eden adventure

Freya, a 2-year-old, is visiting the Eden Project in Cornwall, with her parents. She runs towards a water feature of moving water in shallow channels cut into the paving and she immediately stops and listens. 'I can hear it gurgling and bubbling and . . . giggling down', she calls to her parents. She dips her toes in, splashing in the water, then reaches down to allow the water to run through her fingers; she is fascinated with how it splashes on to the paving and makes handprints with her wet hand, and the water quickly evaporates, as it is a warm day. She spends several minutes exploring making marks in this way. She then collects a pebble and uses this to dam the shallow channel. This causes water to start to emerge over the top of the channel, causing a small puddle; she laughs and goes to get a bigger pebble to add to her dam, and this causes the water to cascade over the paving as it overflows, providing a puddle that she splashes and stamps in, running around, dancing and jumping to make footprints. She is oblivious to the fact that she is being watched, not only by her own parents, but by other adults who have stopped to watch the show, some clearly enjoying it, whereas others 'tut-tut' at the water feature being used as a playground in this way. After a sustained amount of time has been spent in this way, her parents ask her if she would like to play in the sand, and she is taken to a sandpit in a tepee. 'This is the bestest sandpit I've seen, I've never seen one in a tent before.' Her father explains this sort of tent is called a tepee. She plays for several minutes, digging in the sand and giving a constant verbal narration to her play. Another child of similar age enters with her parents. Freya stops digging and goes to stand next to her parents, who are sitting at the edge;

they encourage her to continue to play, but she is reluctant; after several minutes of watching, she sinks down on her knees and begins to dig in silence, but close to her parents; she keeps looking over towards the other child and her family. The two children both dig in isolation from each other, but their actions indicate they are very aware of what each other is doing: as Freya uses a pebble for a door to her castle, the other child asks her Dad for a stone, and, as the other child uses a stick to draw a fence, Freya uses a stick to draw a dog to live in her castle.

This encounter provides us with an interesting account of a child's development, socially, emotionally, physically and cognitively. Let us look first at her play in the water: like Thomas with his objects in the fourth encounter and the child in the oats and sand in the fifth, she uses her senses to explore, finding out what she can do with the water. Her physical mobility allows her to explore using her whole body, as she steps in the water, bends to touch the water and moves spontaneously to make hand- and footprints.

Woods (2006), talks about elemental play, where children discover new ideas and notions through the process of finding out about themselves in relation to their surroundings in the natural environment; she argues that what children are doing is discovering for themselves what man has discovered in the past. This natural instinct to play with the natural elements in the way our earlier ancestors did is referred to as recapitulative play by Hughes (1996). Woods (2006) notes how young children have a strong drive to explore natural elements such as earth, wind, fire and water. In this encounter, Freya was exploring what our ancestors did in earlier evolutionary stages, discovering that watercourses can be changed by creation of a dam.

In this encounter, we see the child using her body, hands and feet to make marks on the paving with the water; she is fully engrossed and in the moment – what Csíkszentmihályi (2001) refers to as a state of flow: the experience itself provides the reward and motivation for the continuation of the activity. She is making marks, and the marks soon evaporate on the paving because it is a warm day, but that is of no concern; the motivation comes from her physical enjoyment. Her marks are not about producing an end product or communicating any meaning, they are just representative of the here and now for her; she is engrossed in epistemic play – 'what does this do?' – and ludic play – 'how can I use this?' (Hutt, 1979, cited in Duffy, 2006). Cecil *et al.* (1985), cited in Duffy (2006: 32), offer a series of four elements in children's creative processes: curiosity, exploration, play and creativity. In this encounter, we see Freya passing through the first three elements, but she does not actually move into creativity. However, a few days later, on returning home from her holiday, she adds soil to a puddle and makes a series of hand- and footprints radiating out, clearly building upon the experience she had with the water feature.

Social play

This extract also provides an example of play with others. Traditionally, theorists have discussed the stages of children's social play, from solitary play in babies, exploring their immediate environment where others are just part of the environment they explore, through to parallel play as children play alongside each other, to associative play, in their third year of life, as children begin to play together but with their own ideas, and, finally, to co-operative play, with shared agendas and narratives to their play. We could describe the play in this extract as that of parallel play, and certainly the age of the children would fit the expected developmental stage for parallel play, but we saw in the third extract the baby of 4 months participating, which was clearly more than the description for solitary play to be expected in a baby of her age. This raises the debate that perhaps children's development through play is not a series of steps, but a complex weaving of the different types of social play, where each new experience adds to a child's future play possibilities. Bruce and Meggitt (1996) describe peer play as a gradually spreading web. If we look at the development of the social play of Freya and the other child using this as a lens, we can see they begin to show interest in what each other is doing and then take on board those ideas in their own play, both as imitation – the use of the pebble for a door – and then as a catalyst for developing their ideas – the stick as a tool for drawing – and it would be interesting to follow this through with further observation. This imitation will be familiar to all those who spend time with young children and can often be seen at group time, when you will often find that the answer the first child gave is then repeated by several others, not necessarily because they do not have their own ideas, but because the first idea has been accepted and assimilated, and, therefore, they imitate it, before fully accommodating the experience alongside other, prior experiences.

The development of language is also worth noting here. In the second encounter, we saw a newborn's interest in voices, in the third, we saw a baby of 4 months wanting to join in communicating, and, in the fourth encounter, Thomas communicated his dissatisfaction, which his carer verbalised for him. Now, at 2 years, we see a child with a command of language, as she gives a constant verbal narration to her play, talking herself through what she is doing; this is often referred to as monologue or internal speech, a precursor to thoughts being internalised, as considered by Vygotsky (1934) discussed in Smidt (2009).

Characteristics of effective learning

In analysing the characteristics of effective learning being demonstrated here, we can see that Freya operates with the following elements:

■ playing and exploring – finding out and exploring: showing curiosity, using her senses, engaging in an open-ended experience and showing interests;

■ playing and exploring – being willing to have a go: initiating activities and engaging in new experiences;

■ active learning – being involved and concentrating: maintaining her focus, high levels of energy and fascination and not being distracted;

■ active learning – enjoying achieving what one sets out to do: enjoying meeting challenges for their own sake, rather than for external reward or praise; and

■ creating and thinking critically – having one's own ideas: thinking of ideas and finding new ways to do things.

Encounter: 'up the centre . . . let's go!'

In a nursery, two boys, one aged 3 and one aged 4, are running in and out of various areas. Boy 1 calls his friend, and they run into the role-play area. They come out dressed in blue jackets and equipped with sunglasses and mobile phones and run to the writing area and find post-it pads and pencils, where they scribble a note; then, outside, they jump on to bikes, pedal a circuit making 'nee naa' sounds and then return inside. As they move through the nursery, snippets of conversation can be heard. 'Up the centre . . . let's go!', 'They are getting away', 'Where did they go?', 'What did they look like?'. The game continues for a sustained period of time, with high energy levels. Several staff members remind the boys not to run indoors, and they briefly stop, but the game is too tempting and exciting and they soon return to running. During the afternoon session, the play continues and develops. The centre they refer to is a local shopping centre; after discussion with the older boy's mother at the end of the day, it becomes clear the pretend play is based on re-enacting and extending a shoplifting scene the older boy had witnessed when shopping the previous day. Pretend play emerges in children in the early part of their second year, once they have developed their understanding of objects (Robinson, 2008), as demonstrated in the encounter Thomas has with his treasure basket. These boys were fully involved in their pretend play and they were playing co-operatively: they had a shared narrative and took turns in leading and following. They were able to collect props they needed to enhance their play and move to various areas in the setting as the narrative story flowed. The play has a common story-telling theme – the good guys chase the bad guys; that they do not have a third child playing the bad guy does not seem to matter – in their minds he is there, and they are chasing him, demonstrating their imaginative skills. This pretending that the something is there, in this case the bad guy, when he is not, is referred to by Vygotsky, cited in Smidt (2009), as decontextualisation of meaning; we also see the boys using what Vygotsky refers to as pre-concepts, using symbols to represent something as they scribble a note on post-it pads after hearing an imaginary description over their mobile phones. Smidt (2009) explains that this is a higher-order concept. We also see elements of planning for the play, as the boys equip themselves with the tools a police officer needs before the play commences. Robinson (2008: 141) cites the work of Zelazo *et al.* (2003), where they describe different types of thinking as 'executive functions, processes that are involved in the conscious control of thought and action with related skills and abilities . . . planning, problem solving and self-monitoring'.

The children in the seventh encounter demonstrate many of the characteristics of effective learning:

- playing and exploring – playing with what they know: pretending that objects are things from their experience, representing their experiences in play, taking on a role in their play, acting out their experiences with other people;
- active learning – being involved and concentrating: maintaining a focus on their activity for a period of time, showing high levels of energy, paying attention to details; and
- creating and thinking critically – choosing ways to do things: planning and making decisions.

Encounter: building a den

A mixed Years 1 and 2 class is involved in a forest school session in the school grounds. The children have been given time to follow their own lines of enquiry after an initial discussion. Three girls have decided to work together; they want to create a den. Girl 1 takes the initiative, asking the others where they should build and what style den they should make (the previous week's session included activities on shelter building). The others make suggestions, and together they negotiate where they will site their den and what style they will use. Girls 2 and 3 go off to collect branches, while Girl 1 stays to 'guard our spot so nobody else comes here'. They have chosen an area that is already partly sheltered by the boundary of the school site and under a large horse chestnut tree, which they use as a central support. The den making progresses well; when a small section collapses, they scream, but then decide they need longer branches, and soon they have a finished structure and they all crawl inside. Girl 3 decides it is too damp and goes off to collect a tarpaulin, which she then lays as a carpet in their den. Further modifications are made, as Girl 3 decides to weave long grass and twigs between the large branches they have used, and Girls 1 and 2 join in with this. Girl 1 suggests they make a name for their den, and together they come up with a name they are all happy with and write it, using a stick, in the soft earth outside the den. Throughout the den building, there is a constant dialogue about the task in hand, but also about what classmates are doing.

In this encounter, we can see the progression in the use of the executive functions from the previous encounter. Executive functions begin to develop towards the end of a child's first year and continue to develop, with children having the potential for rapid development in these skills between the age of 3 and 5 (Centre on the Developing Child at Harvard University, 2011). The roots of executive functions lie in the prefrontal cortex of the brain but require different regions of the brain to work together. In this encounter, we see the girls coming together to form a plan; as they plan, they use what is described by the Centre on the Developing Child at Harvard University (2011) as their working memory: they draw on learning the previous week and apply it to the task in hand. We also see them able to respond with mental flexibility, adapting plans when there is a setback and the den collapses. Open-ended experiences such as those described in the eighth encounter are rich opportunities for the development of the executive functions, which are essential life skills.

This encounter also sees how the girls are able to work together and maintain their focus when there are external distractions. They are fully aware of what other groups are doing, but do not let them influence their plans, nor do they respond to them in any way; this inhibitory control is a further executive function.

The girls in this encounter demonstrate many of the characteristics of effective learning:

- playing and exploring – being willing to have a go: they show a can-do attitude, even with setbacks, and learn by trial and error;
- active learning – being involved and concentrating: maintaining a focus on their activity for a period of time, showing high levels of energy, and not being distracted;
- active learning – keep on trying: persisting as challenges occur and bouncing back after difficulties;
- active learning – enjoying achieving what they set out to do: meeting challenges and being intrinsically motivated;
- creating and thinking critically – having their own ideas: planning and solving problems; and
- creating and thinking critically – choosing ways to do things: planning and making decisions to reach their goal of building a den, changing strategy as needed and reviewing their approach.

As we have seen, child development is best viewed as a coming together, as biological and emotional factors emerge and unfold in our experiences of people, places and things, leading us to challenge previous ideas and develop new skills, interests and ways of doing things.

A final encounter, observed by a local authority adviser for early years, takes us back to the opening of this chapter, where it is suggested that children are naturally playful and have a desire to want to play.

> ## Encounter: let me play!
>
> In a mixed Reception and Years 1 and 2 class, in a small village school, a reception-age boy has given up doing his phonics worksheet that he can neither read nor understand. He takes a car from his pocket and begins to use the edge of his paper as a racetrack; he gradually becomes more involved, making noises and using other items on the desk as props. The teacher calls over to his table to tidy up; he makes no attempt to do this and, as she walks over to check on progress, he crawls under the desk and continues to play; she doesn't notice him and takes the others off to the whiteboard to carry out a phonics activity, and he continues to play cars under the desk.

Watching this encounter was heart wrenching – his play with the car was much more developmentally appropriate and involved more of the characteristics of effective learning than the worksheet activity. This offers us a word of caution when we consider what is developmentally appropriate for this child at this point in time; if we do this, we should feel confident that they will be able to display the characteristics of effective learning. We should also remember that the most important resource is an adult with a sound knowledge of child development, tuned in to respond appropriately to the child.

Provocations

- How much do you know about child development, including brain development? Do you know how children learn to master skills such as crawling and talking, which they may have achieved before they come to you? How do you use this knowledge? How do you keep abreast of research into child development?

- Do you and your colleagues discuss child development? Do you talk about individual children in relation to their holistic development, or do your discussions tend to focus on curricular targets and planned learning intentions?

- Consider your relationships with parents: how do you encourage them to share encounters or observations from home that will enhance your knowledge of their child's personal development? Do you ask about earlier stages in their child's development and use these as a lens to understand the child you know? Do you share your observations and use your knowledge of child development to explain a child's behaviour or play to parents?

- Do your relationships with other professionals provide you with space and time to discuss together children who may not be following typical development patterns?

- When planning, do you consider the individual child's development prior to the curriculum and whole-group planning?

References

Blott, M. (2009) *The Day-By-Day Pregnancy Book*. London: Dorling Kindersley.

Bruce, T. and Meggitt, C. (1996) *Childcare and Education*. London: Hodder & Stoughton.

Bruner, J. (1983) *Child's Talk: Learning to Use Language*. Oxford, UK: Oxford University Press.

Centre on the Developing Child at Harvard University (2011) *Building the Brain's 'Air Traffic Control' System: How Early Experiences Shape the Development of Executive Function: Working Paper 11*. Available online at: www.developingchild.harvard.edu (accessed 30 December 2013).

Chomsky, N. (1965) *Aspects of a Theory of Syntax*. Cambridge, MA: MIT Press.

Csíkszentmihályi, M. (2001) *Beyond Boredom and Anxiety: Experiencing Flow in Work and Play*. San Francisco, CA: Jossey-Bass.

Duffy, B. (2006) *Supporting Creativity and Imagination in the Early Years*, 2nd edn. Maidenhead, UK: Open University Press.

Forbes, R. (2004) *Beginning to Play: Young Children From Birth to Three*. Maidenhead, UK: Open University Press.

Goddard Blythe, S. (2005) *The Well-Balanced Child: Movement and Early Learning*. Stroud, UK: Hawthorn Press.

Gopnik, A., Meltzoff, A. and Kuhl, P. (1999) *How Babies Think*. London: Phoenix.

Hughes, B. (1996) *A Playworker's Taxonomy of Play Types*. London: Playlink.

Karmiloff, K. and Karmiloff-Smith, A. (2001) *Pathways to Language: From Foetus to Adolescent*. Cambridge, MA: Harvard University Press.

Laevers, F. (1994) *The Leuven Scale for Young Children*. Belgium: Centre for Experiential Education.

Manning-Morton, J. and Thorpe, M. (2001) *Key Times: A Framework for Developing High Quality Provision for Children under Three Years*. London: Camden EYDCP/University of North London.

Murray, A. and Andrews, E. (2000) *Social Baby*. London: Richmond Press.

Robinson, M. (2008) *Child Development 0–8*. Maidenhead, UK: Open University Press.

Smidt, S. (2009) *Introducing Vygotsky*. Abingdon, UK: Routledge.

Woods, A. (2006) *The Magic Chocolate Pit: A Story to Illustrate Elemental Play*, paper presented at ARECE Conference, Melbourne, January.

2

Exploring children's well-being and motivations

Lorna Wardle and Sharon Vesty

The encounters considered in Chapter 1 gave us an illustration of children who exhibit high levels of well-being and involvement in a range of experiential contexts. Much has been written about well-being in relation to attachment theory, emotional health and the nurturing of both young children and maturing adults; in essence, that well-being is fundamental to a person's assured social and emotional relations, as well as physical health. Well-being can be a confusing concept for many professionals and parents, and, when the concept is explored through published guidance, literature and practitioner advice, it ranges from happiness and contentment to resilience and motivation, all intrinsic characteristics where their *absence* is a sign of low well-being; their presence is much more elusive to define. We can, however, usually recognise relaxation, expression of interest, pleasure, energy, flexibility and an inner contentedness, with self-motivated activity, as well as participation and willingness to approach and work with others, both adults and children, in situations that meet their needs. These characteristics, for us, define well-being.

Within this chapter, we discuss how practitioners become attuned to levels of well-being in children as well as help children tune into themselves, and we use Podmore *et al.*'s interpretation of the five aspirations for children's well-being (2001), as set out in the *Te Whāriki* curriculum documentation (New Zealand Ministry of Education, 1996); these are well-being, belonging, contribution, communication and exploration. This tool helps us to investigate the child–practitioner dynamic and how children's characteristics of learning depend upon a high level of well-being. The interpretative aspirations here are included as questions from the child's perspective and help us to consider our role as adults.

We need to have some clarity on the concept of well-being when working with children in order to assess, observe and monitor them. In the past decade, the UK government has valued the importance of supporting and enhancing children's well-being from the introduction of *Every Child Matters* (Department for Children, Schools and Families, 2003) through to the Early Years Foundation Stage (EYFS) (Department for Education, 2012) framework, which promotes characteristics of learning, whereby well-being and motivation play a major role. Sections 3.6, 3.20, 3.25 and 3.52 of the EYFS statutory framework clearly identify the requirement for early practitioners to have regard for and promote children's well-being, going beyond the difficult 'achieve economic well-being' when applied to young children.

Well-being: can I trust you?

Laevers (2002: 5) defines well-being as 'show[ing] us how much the educational environment succeeds in helping the child *to feel at home* [our italics], to be her/himself, to remain in contact with her/himself and have her/his emotional needs (the need for attention, recognition, competence . . .) fulfilled'. The Department of Health (2009: 8) further describes well-being as 'a dynamic state, in which the individual is able to develop their potential, work productively and creatively, build strong and positive relationships with others, and contribute to their community'.

Dubnoff (1970: 37) suggests that 'children [can] "fall apart" repeatedly but unlike Humpty Dumpty, grow together again', and Erikson's psychosocial theory (cited in Mooney, 2000) outlines infant and lifelong development through a series of crises to be overcome during identifiable developmental stages. Erikson's analysis of troubled adults led him to trace back early and unresolved episodes they had experienced and theorise that a means to resolve the issue was to engender a feeling of 're-parenting' for the client. Resolution of lifespan crises or challenges and the ability to resolve them oneself appear to be part of developing a strong sense of well-being; success at resolution will then feed future motivation and self-confidence. Erikson stated that, in the first stage of infancy, the period from birth to 18 months, he saw the child as dependent on the parents and carers, with the key developmental challenge at this stage related to trust and mistrust. The child learns to trust their main carers, who are their world and provide for all their needs. When this does not happen, mistrust can develop, and the child becomes anxious, thereby affecting their well-being and self-esteem. Carers play a large part in supporting the child's well-being by ensuring effective communication and unconditional love, with close attachments, within the child's microsystem or immediate close family and community, sharing knowledge of likes, dislikes, favourite toys and routines. Effective and nurturing transitional arrangements between home and setting are needed, therefore, to ensure that the trust is secure between parent and practitioner, child and practitioner and child and parent. The parent needs to trust the setting to love their child unconditionally, as they do; the parent also needs to feel that the practitioners are working with them, rather than judging or working against them. The child will sense this partnership and also recognise, as Laevers (2002) states, that they *feel at home* and looked after, an experience already gained with their primary carer.

Offering an early breakfast for all children as part of a welcome may be part of an everyday nursery and school routine. Maslow (1954) suggested that basic human survival needs must be met before self-esteem can be developed. Practitioners relate to this theory within childcare and educational settings and recognise that children have to have their basic needs met in order to sustain the well-being required to learn and actively participate within the nursery day.

Encounter: providing breakfast

The manager of a day nursery recognised that children accessing care provision appeared lethargic, disinterested and unmotivated until after the mid-morning snack was provided, when she observed an increase in their attention span and participation. She recognised that the children might be hungry and acknowledged the impact of not being provided breakfast at home and starting nursery with the basic need of food not being provided. With this in mind, she adapted the nursery opening hours by 15 minutes first thing in the morning, offering breakfast for all the children.

Consequently, the children participated and engaged with the environment at the beginning of the morning session, rather than not engaging until after snack time. With the new regime, the manager reflected that the children were more able to access resources and be involved in activities, with concentration and learning at a deeper level taking place. This reveals how the theory of Maslow's hierarchy of needs can be applied successfully to a child's development and well-being, and how any early years setting can be adapted to support well-being by using one simple measure. It also acknowledges the importance of practitioners needing to tune into children by observing their behaviour and adapting the nursery regime to meet specific needs.

Encounter: April's transition and continuity

A 16-month-old child who is normally happy and content to attend nursery is mildly unwell with a cold. The parent observes the child being quieter than usual and holding on to a soft toy (monkey) that normally provides her with comfort at bedtime. The mother discusses the change in the child's behaviour with the nursery staff, stressing the importance of the soft toy. The child's key person actively listens

---

to the mother and tunes into both the parent's and child's needs. The key person applies a flexible approach to the needs of the family and encourages the parent to leave the monkey with her. The child is then able to self-sooth by holding the monkey, as and when she needs comfort throughout the day.

This encounter demonstrates that April's carers were willing to ensure that they supported her when she was not feeling well by exchanging key information and meeting the child's needs, with a very simple solution of allowing the child to hold on to the 'special monkey'. Transitional objects (Winnicott, 1965) are very important and played a major part in this encounter. The monkey, as a transitional object, provided comfort for the child and a reminder of her mother, creating a sense of comfort while she was feeling unwell. The issue of transitional objects can be a challenging one for settings where the possession/loss/sharing of precious belongings can present difficulties. A setting can use a basket where children are encouraged to place their objects, in view of the child, where they are safe, available if and when needed, but afforded the important role that they play. This comfort support and nurture help to provide an environment and culture whereby the child's well-being is supported and, in turn, increased. A further important factor in this encounter is that April has a key worker present at the nursery, with whom she has also built trust and by whom she is happy to be comforted, in the absence of the parent. Bowlby (2007) uses the term secondary attachment figure and believes that it is absolutely essential that continuity of personalised caregiving is available to babies and toddlers at all times, either from their primary attachment figure or from a trusted secondary attachment figure. A child associates the feeling of well-being with the tuning in and consistent behaviour of the carers and practitioners.

The key-person system is an advocated method in early years settings, where caring personal relationships are developed between practitioners and children. Elfer *et al.* (2003) identify that it has clear benefits for the child, staff and family and offers an opportunity for children to learn and develop stable, close relationships with individual practitioners. By building these close relationships, children form warm, secure bonds with practitioners who really know and understand them *and can be trusted*. Children also need to be encouraged and nurtured by an extended group of adults in the setting, should there be a key worker absence.

Support towards improving and maintaining a child's well-being is the practitioner's role when managing the transition of the child within new settings, changes in routine and situations and new relationships. As well-being includes emotional health, children need to be ready to cope with transitions in the early years. Many children may suffer stress or anxiety in a new situation, where there is a change to routine, which can have a negative effect on their well-being. The child may become withdrawn and show resistance to joining in and forming relationships. The practitioner should observe any changes to the child's state of well-being and respond appropriately. The impact of effectively managing the transition will have a positive effect on the child's ability to cope and manage change themselves, therefore improving well-being and motivating the child to continue to join in and be able to learn within the setting. Coping with change is an important life skill that children need experience of and support with throughout child- to adulthood.

Belonging: do you know me?

Encounter: Imran eating fruit

A 2-year-old child is being offered a plate of orange segments. The child is reluctant to come to the table where the plate is, and the practitioner is waiting; however, the child continues to stand by another table on her own. He attempts to coax the child to the table, but she gets distressed and will not move away from where she is standing. The practitioner talks and listens to the child and gives her the freedom to choose where she wants to sit by giving her the plate of fruit. The child then sits down at the table of her choice and happily eats the fruit.

Lee *et al.* (2013) view well-being as children experiencing an environment where they can develop and are given the opportunity to help themselves, where their individual nutrition and other needs and preferences are being catered for appropriately. Lee *et al.* (2013) ask the rhetorical question – do you meet my daily needs with care and sensitive consideration?

Within this encounter, the practitioner has tuned into Imran and has given freedom of choice and permission to the child to decide where she eats her fruit. Although boundaries are set within the environment, the practitioner sensitively allows the child to make a decision, therefore showing her that she has a choice. The practitioner shows that she knows what will help Imran.

Encounter: snack bar

Staff in a toddler room adapted their routine and continuous provision by providing a snack bar system for the children, set up each day. A table was set up with a small jug of water, cups and plastic containers with a variety of snacks and small plates. Children could independently access this table at any point throughout the session, when they were hungry or thirsty. This promoted self-help, independence and self-care skills for eating and drinking. The early years practitioners recognised that this provided the freedom for children to make a choice, rather than dictating snack times for the children.

Here again, in this encounter, the practitioners appear to *know* the children, their readiness to make decisions for themselves and their ability to service their own needs. Feeling a sense of belonging and sensing consistent boundaries contribute to a state of well-being and can be seen within Roberts' well-being model (2010), where physical development, communication, boundaries and belonging form part of a 'well-being pyramid'. Boundaries are an important aspect of belonging and are where the practitioner communicates to the child a set of unspoken or spoken expectations. In order to improve well-being, the communication also needs to be two-way, where a practitioner listens, watches and acknowledges the child's needs; reciprocally, the child also needs to feel comfortable and confident to express their own needs and wants, while accepting an adult's perspective, questions and responses. Fitting in with others and forming relationships that are meaningful allow the child freedom to express themselves and the practitioner to allow the child to 'fly', but still meet their needs with sensitivity and consideration. In order for learning to take place, we need to challenge children to push their boundaries and zone of proximal development, communicate with us and gain independence. Children need to make decisions and, at times, face difficult choices or struggles whereby they find a solution and resolve a situation for themselves and in doing so create a positive self-confidence and well-being. A practitioner who reinforces that a child has made a good decision will motivate both a child's metacognition and also the willingness to repeat this successful strategy.

Communication: do you hear me?

Not only do children need to have a positive relationship with those closest to them, they also need, and deserve, to feel respected by adults and their peers, as Moran (in Woods, 2013: 38) states: 'In settings, practitioners who respect children's rights will observe their actions, tuning into all their ways of communicating their preferences, interests and fascinations'. This concept is understood by many early years practitioners. Adopting elements of the Reggio Emilia approach, children are seen as unique subjects, with rights rather than simply needs (Rinaldi, 2006). Moran further argues:

> A perception of each child as competent in the eyes of the practitioner empowers all children to have a voice. Careful attention will need to be employed in order to hear the voice of those children who struggle to make their voice heard. This applies to children with additional needs of all kinds and, again, should include the voice of parents to ensure the fullest possible view of the child. Some children may be isolated by language (delayed development or a first language other than that of the setting), culture, faith or ethnicity, gender, ability or disability. Some children present as quiet

within the setting and avoid being recipients of attention, preferring the background to centre stage.

(Woods, 2013: 39)

Focusing on how children appear and how they engage with their environment is a key role for all early years professionals. Tuning in to young children is of paramount importance for understanding their individual characteristics, needs, expressions and interests. The practitioner observes children on a daily basis and historically has a duty to acknowledge those skills that the children are learning; however, it is essential that we look into the characteristics of effective learning and acknowledge whether the children are involved or engaged within the environment. When age and stages of development are supported effectively, practitioners work together with children to build on and extend children's knowledge, skills and competencies. In Chapter 7, Brown explores how sustained thinking and conversations ensure that effective learning takes place, and yet the ability to *hear* children is greater than active listening. It is worth considering the ways in which children are afforded the opportunity to express their ideas, choices, interests, plans and projects; how babies' engagement and curiosity are enhanced, and how often children guide the curriculum and create their own learning spaces within the environment provided; how we consult children over routines and changes; and the length of time we give to children to explain, question, discuss and philosophise. Given these opportunities, we can be confident that our children will be 'ready, willing and able' and motivated to be active participants, with an assured level of well-being.

Contribution: is this place fair for me?

Education and care settings have a significant impact on children's well-being. Young children need the conditions to explore, learn and develop, and high-quality learning environments, both indoors and outside, are key to supporting children. Adult attention and interaction are vital while children are participating in these experiences and will have a positive impact on well-being by increasing a child's sense of worth. Learning can be seen as a process of social construction, whereby a child learns in relationship with others (Rinaldi, 2006). The Effective Provision of Pre-School Education Project (Sylva *et al.*, 2004) found that a high-quality preschool experience is related to better social, behavioural and intellectual development, suggesting that children made more progress in settings where practitioners displayed warm adult–child interaction and responded to children's individual needs.

Laevers (2002) designed a well-being and involvement scale to show us how to measure levels of well-being in order that, as practitioners, we can begin to distinguish between superficial and deep-level learning and how the educational environment can be effective and, crucially, articulate those elements of quality that support a child's well-being. Building a collaborative relationship is essential to support children to feel respected and valued.

We know as adults that, when we are tired, uncomfortable and hungry or anxious, our motivation and well-being decrease; therefore, we must apply this knowledge to children and address these issues to increase well-being, because children may only *show us* rather than be able to tell us. It is paramount that practitioners embrace a social pedagogy as described by Petrie (2011) – 'the 3 Ps': the professional, the personal and the private. As practitioners, we recognise that we need to show our professional knowledge skills and attitudes in work; however, in order to maintain our own well-being, we need to see ourselves as people too, and not be afraid to express feelings. Sharing these feelings ensures congruence, empathy and unconditional positive regard towards the child and allows the child to do the same, which in turn supports their well-being. Settings need to not only focus on child development, but also to provide opportunities for practitioner development, to ensure that our attention and approaches are received by all children in our care. Practitioners need to be adaptable with their expectations for children, so that they learn to cope in different situations.

We need to apply our observations and adapt our practice to stimulate children's interest, concentration and attention within the learning environment. Play experiences are an ideal way for children to express their feelings in a safe environment and a means by which children find stimulation, well-being and pleasure. White (2002) states that children need an understanding of feelings themselves, and, here, the role of the practitioner is to support children to learn, understand and manage their feelings through play, thus supporting the children's need to develop an understanding of how their behaviour and expressions impact on themselves and others. They also have a role in establishing fair and just boundaries, respect for each other and a 'helping ethos', to enable children to move from the self to empathising with others.

Giving praise to children is an important factor in supporting motivation within a learning context. Genuine praise for their efforts and achievement will encourage the child to develop their own inner balance and confidence. Recognising children's efforts and achievement, and not praising constantly, where praise can seem meaningless, allows the child to accept that they are able to make mistakes and then manage these. Erikson (1963) implies that children may have to accept artificial bolstering of their self-esteem, but their ego-identity gains real strength only from whole-hearted and consistent recognition of real accomplishment.

Encounter: positive encouragement

A 10-month-old infant is playing with a plastic cookie jar and putting shapes into the jar and taking them out. Whenever she has put in all the shapes, the parents clap and give praise. When this happens, the child's face beams, and immediately she starts to do the task again. Subsequently, each time she has put a shape into the jar, she looks for the parents' recognition of her achievement and their attention. The parents respond by giving praise for the task and encourage the child to continue until all the shapes are back in the cookie jar.

This encounter reveals that we need to examine the role of genuine praise in order to support the child to develop their self-esteem and confidence. Skinner (1968: 10) suggested that, if we constantly praise children for learning or behaving in a certain way, they will behave in the same way again, thus creating conditions 'which are optimal for producing the changes called learning'. A further way of demonstrating high regard for a child is by praising them both to peers, thus encouraging a 'ripple effect' in a setting in order that children can recognise good learning and behaviour, and also to a parent, within the child's hearing, enhancing the 'feel-good' and well-being of the family.

Vygotsky (1962) suggested that the child could learn independently and be moved on by their knowledge through interaction with someone with a greater level of knowledge and experience. Within the previous encounter, both theories can be applied, to both praising the behaviour but also interacting with the child to show them how to put the shapes into the cookie jar in different ways. Relating this to the *Te Whāriki* approach (New Zealand Ministry of Education, 1996), we consider both the exploration and communication aspirations for children. We understand that, through the interaction with the child and the cookie jar, the parent is both observing a level of well-being and is instrumental in developing the child's self-confidence and self-esteem. Through this quality interaction, the child is motivated to be a competent and confident learner.

Cowie *et al.* (2013) describe the physical and psychosocial environment, in and around school, and how it plays a crucial role in creating a positive ethos. The environment is not only visual, but should also offer a secure, safe place for emotional development. This implies a positive ethos for all children, in order that children sense and see that the setting is *fair*.

Encounter: child with no voice

A teaching assistant (TA) in a classroom is dealing with administrative tasks and is unable to give a child their full attention. The child wanted the TA to see his work, but the TA responded three times with 'in a minute'. The child went to a writing table and drew a picture of a very small person on an A4 piece of paper. When the TA asked the child to tell her about the picture, the 5-year-old child responded with, 'That's how I feel when you ignore me'.

Within this encounter, the child has voiced the impact of how the TA made him feel when she was not paying attention and repeatedly putting other tasks before the child's needs. It may be that the TA was setting boundaries for the child, to help him be more independent, but explanations need to be explicit and fair, and the encounter rather suggests that the adult was not fully engaged as a work/play companion for the child.

Encounter: developing identity

A 4-year-old boy chose to wear a dress for the whole nursery session; however, after tea, towards the end of the session, when he knew his parent would be collecting him, he would take off the dress, ensuring that he was not wearing it when he saw his parent. This child showed he had the confidence to express himself and trust the practitioners in the setting.

This child had the self-confidence to express himself and enthusiastically tell his friends and practitioners that he enjoyed wearing the dress and seemed content to be developing his own identity, which appeared not to reflect his peers' behaviour. The motivation of the child to be different was encouraged by the choices offered by practitioners. Managing this awareness and expression indicates that the child's self-confidence was high. Making choices in this way shows good levels of well-being, whereby his daily needs were met by the practitioners with sensitivity and consideration, therefore playing a major part in the child being able to trust the practitioner and feel that the setting was fair for him. The practitioners here need to find a way to bridge any gap between the child's perception of his parents' possible reaction to his wearing a dress and their actual reaction, when he seems to be aware that his behaviour was 'different', and be able to explore with them his growing sense of identity. Well-being in this encounter is demonstrating a child's need to have his emotional and psychological needs met, and, if this is related to Maslow's (1954) theory, it has moved from his physical needs to the higher, emotional needs and working towards self-esteem.

Exploration: do you let me fly?

Children recognised as competent learners need opportunities for open-ended exploration (see the Chapters 4 and 6 by Woods and Gripton) and the possibility to learn from others. Early years practitioners need to provide children with opportunities to share and demonstrate their knowledge with their peers and create an environment for children to share their competencies and to also enable inspired learning. As children interact with others, they learn to take risks, think critically and problem solve.

Malaguzzi's (1998) pedagogical approach promotes the image of the competent, confident child, rich in potential, strong and powerful, connected to adults and to other children. Children are viewed as co-constructors of knowledge, learning alongside their peers and adults.

Encounter: recognising a child's zone of proximal development

A 3-year-old boy is playing in the playground and attempting to walk along a rope on the climbing frame, being guided by his parents. The frustration at his parents' constant guidance and reassurance was evident; however, on the last part of the climbing frame, the 3-year-old boy was able to manoeuvre the tightrope with side ropes himself. Extreme concentration and focus were required, but, in the end, he successfully manoeuvred along the rope to the end. Upon looking up at his parents, his facial expression was one of sheer joy, accomplishment and pride in the fact that he had managed this task on his own. The boy looked for praise and reassurance from the parents that he had achieved an important goal.

Encounter: enabling a child's zone of proximal development

Two-year-old Harry is climbing up the toddler slide in the playground and getting to the top, but is hesitant to slide down. The nursery worker is coaxing the child to explore the top and look over, sit at the top of the slide and then, eventually, when ready, slide down. After many times of repeating these actions, he gradually climbed up the steps, went to the top, sat down and then went down the slide alone. Once the child had done it on his own, the realisation of having achieved this task showed in the child's face, and he then became confident at repeating the task more quickly and more easily, without the nursery worker needing to coax further.

Within these encounters, the parents and practitioner used both praise and encouragement to motivate the children to explore the rope and slide. The children's motivation was fostered and supported by the constant reassurance and praise, recognising that the children were doing well. This approach demonstrates both the parents and practitioner offering the children the opportunity of challenge at the boundaries of their comfort zone; the children were learning about themselves by doing, being active, practising and repeating activity through interactions (Rogoff, 1990).

When people praise us, and we show delight in our expression, it is often because we are filled with happiness that we have pleased the other person. In the encounter, the motivation came from within the child, with a need to complete the task and receive praise from the adult. Recognising that he had done well and would receive praise from the adult gave Harry the motivation to repeat the task again and again. Much like an adult would gain a sense of achievement from successfully completing a task, the satisfaction would be seen by all around by their delight at the achievement. The child picks up these signals, and, therefore, well-being is increased by the achievement. When children demonstrate this satisfaction to others, Laevers (1994) describes it as making new connections within the affective and/or cognitive domain, therefore demonstrating that, when they feel a sense of achievement by taking the lead and mastering skills, the characteristics of learning are accompanied with a deep sense of intensity and satisfaction.

Well-being that is fostered and supported by motivation and praise is vital to the development and sustenance of learning dispositions. The impact on learning from being praised as a child continues throughout our development and life. Children preserve their self-esteem by experiencing a sense of achievement that then helps to develop and maintain their self-worth (Glazzard et al., 2010). Allowing children to manage 'good' risks and expose themselves to challenges is important for their confidence and self-esteem and, in addition, their emotional and mental well-being (Edgington 2007).

When children have a good sense of well-being, they feel the freedom to explore and push their own skills and boundaries, enabling them to build upon their self-worth, as part of their well-being. Praise encourages children to do this and, coupled with the developing learning dispositions, ensures that they know their own progress and development. Children experience their learning achievements from people and events, at school, within the family and among friends (Smyth, 2013), therefore, practitioners working with children have an important role in fostering favourable conditions that facilitate children's growth. It is imperative that the environment allows this freedom of choice: open-ended activity, choice of resources, prolonged time to explore interests, opportunity both to make and resolve mistakes, and making connections will inevitably create favourable conditions for characteristics of effective learning and the development of robust learning dispositions, as examined in Chapter 4.

Self-reliance also plays a part in the development of a child's well-being and needs to be nurtured and enabled by practitioners who model this themselves. Children learn by exploring and, as practitioners, we must allow them freedom to experience independence. We know that a child's needs will change with different situations and different times of day, and we must be able to read and be sensitive to the child's transient well-being. A child who feels tired or unwell will require additional support and comfort in order to maintain independence, motivation and overall well-being.

Encounter: intrinsic motivation

Mary, who is 18 months old, is sitting by herself and playing with a set of plastic saucepans. One saucepan has a lid that fits on it perfectly, and Mary is trying to put the lid on to the various saucepans. At first, she tries to put the lid on to the two smaller saucepans but, seeing it will not fit, she then turns to the third saucepan, which is the correct saucepan for the lid. Mary sits very quietly on her own, turning the lid around to attempt to fit it to the saucepan perfectly. She is totally engrossed in this task; sometimes the lid goes inside the pan, other times she puts it on but it falls off. Mary continues to attempt this task for 5 minutes, just sitting on her own, determined to get the lid on to the saucepan correctly. Finally, the lid snaps perfectly into place on the pan, and Mary knows that this is the right fit. At this point, she looks up and sees that there is an adult observing her, and so she smiles and starts to clap herself. The practitioner joins in with the clapping and praises Mary.

This encounter displays the child's intrinsic motivation, whereby Mary continues to carry out the task until she had completed it and it 'felt right'. The practitioner gave Mary the quiet time and space to complete the task, without taking over and showing her how to do it. From this encounter, we can see where motivation to complete a task comes from when there is no one praising or motivating the child to undertake or complete the task. Some of these learning skills come naturally, such as exploring, questioning and experimenting; however, children need to be able to make mistakes and keep trying until they themselves solve the problem or complete the task. Often, as practitioners, we have a desire or need to step in and demonstrate how it is done or take control of the situation. If we allow the child the time and permission to try things out, then they will be successful in learning new skills and, importantly, gain a sense of satisfaction. Children are given praise and encouragement to support external motivation whereby they achieve the right way do things, but intrinsic motivation comes from the need to explore, investigate, ask questions and have opportunities to answer their own questions and complete their own tasks (Robins, 2012). This intrinsic motivation will lead to more effective learning, where the child has an internal drive to learn.

Cohen (1972) describes the locus of a young child's confidence as not in the thinking but in their solar plexus, in the sense of themselves as an active learner who has an awareness of feelings and being. Within the encounter, Mary has learned to keep on trying, which will lead to a sense of deep self-satisfaction and a sense of achievement and pride. This was shown by Mary lifting her head and smiling at the practitioner, once she had completed the task, and then gaining the praise that she welcomed. This is an example of intrinsic motivation, which comes from within the mind of each person, allowing them to learn to enjoy a challenge, in the knowledge that they can reach a positive outcome and receive praise and self-assurance. Mary appeared self-motivated within this encounter and initially did not need external motivation or approval, but only her own mastery of a skill. Children who display internal motivation will often not need the approval of other children or adults, but see them as people who encourage them to set and reach their own targets. The practitioner in the encounter provided Mary with the time and space to undertake the playful learning and, therefore, achieve the point that felt right for her.

A highly motivated child will demonstrate high levels of involvement for a lengthy period of time, whereas an unmotivated child's levels of involvement will be low, and the child will be easily be distracted from the task in hand. Children who demonstrate the characteristic of persistence are often successfully engaged in the activity or experience. Key motivators for persistence are courage, curiosity and challenge. In order to sustain the desire to experience challenge and uncertainty, children must first have the opportunity to experience success. Practitioners need to plan opportunities for children to achieve realistic next steps. As a child is successful with their achievement, they begin to develop an awareness and understanding of satisfaction, and, therefore, motivational learning will develop.

Motivations for each child will vary, but one common characteristic for children's motivation is enjoyment. Motivated children will often feel a high level of enjoyment in their activity or experience. Without pleasure in their activity, children's levels of well-being and involvement will often decrease, and intrinsic motivation will not be demonstrated. Many of us know that children learn best when they are having fun, but we often are task driven, rather than planning and allowing simple enjoyment.

The characteristic of inquisitiveness will be demonstrated by the child who wants to explore and learn, and they may have a fascination with people, places or things, or all three. Through intrinsic motivation, the child has no obvious concern with an external reward; instead, the child will ask thoughtful questions, as they apply sustained shared thinking with others. Motivations play a major part in a child's well-being, through allowing both intrinsic and extrinsic factors to enhance the child's confidence, self-esteem and overall development through to adulthood.

Practitioner perspectives

As practitioners, we would do well to consider the questions posed by the *Te Whāriki* curriculum (New Zealand Ministry of Education, 1996), not only from the child's perspective, but for ourselves: if we feel we belong, we are known and recognised for who we are and could be; we are trusted and trust our colleagues; we abide by fair and valued judgements and can express our new or alternative ideas without criticism or discrimination; it should follow then that our environment will be a place where our children sense these qualities also. An environment where they want to join in, look forward to and enjoy challenge will be a place for me, us and the children – a place of well-being and effective learning.

Provocations

- As a practitioner, can you describe well-being in children to a colleague or parent?
- Can you give examples of children who have good well-being and poor well-being?
- When do you listen to and value children's voices and opinions? How are children consulted within your establishment?
- How do you listen to children without spoken dialogue?
- Can you think of ways that professionals can foster and improve well-being in children with whom they work?
- In what ways could you work with a parent to raise a family's well-being?
- Can you think of a time when you have praised a child and it has had a positive effect?
- Think of those children who apparently present no concerns – how have/do you promote and develop their well-being?
- How do you support young children through transitional events?
- How do you help young children feel a sense of belonging within your early years environment?

References

Bowlby, R. (2007) Babies and toddlers in non-parental day-care can avoid stress and anxiety if they develop a lasting secondary attachment bond with one carer who is consistently accessible to them. *Attachment & Human Development* 9(4): 318.

Cohen, D. (1972) *The Learning Child*. London: Random House.

Cowie, H., Boardman, C., Dawkins, J. and Jennifer, D. (2013) *Emotional Health and Well-being*. London: Sage.

Department for Children, Schools and Families (2003) *Every Child Matters*. London: The Stationery Office.

Department for Education (2012) *Statutory Framework for the Early Years Foundation Stage (EYFS)*. Cheshire, UK: Department for Education.

Department of Health (2009) *New Horizons: A Shared Vision for Mental Health*. London: HM Government.

Dubnoff, B. (1970) Building ego factors through the curriculum. *Journal of Learning Disabilities* 3(459): 36–42.

Edgington, M. (2007) Supporting young children to engage with risk and challenge. *Early Years: International Journal of Research and Development* 27(2).

Elfer, P. Goldschmied, E. and Selleck, D. (2003) *Key Persons in the Nursery: Building Relationships for Quality Provision*. London: David Fulton.

Erikson, E. (1963) *Childhood and Society*, 2nd edn. New York: Norton.

Glazzard, J., Chadwick, D., Webster, A. and Percival, J. (2010) *Assessment for Learning in the Early Years Foundation Stage*. London: Sage.

Laevers, F. (ed.) (1994) *The Leuven Involvement Scale for Young Children*. LIS-YC Manual. Leuven, Belgium: Centre for Experiential Education.

Laevers, F. (2002) *Research on Experiential Education: A Selection of Articles*. Leuven, Belgium: Centre for Experiential Education.

Lee, W. Carr, M., Soutar, B. and Mitchell, L. (2013) *Understanding the Te Whāriki Approach*. Abingdon, UK: Routledge.

Malaguzzi, L. (1998) History, ideas and basic philosophy. In Edwards, C.P., Gandini, L. and Forman, G. (eds) *The Hundred Languages of Children: The Reggio Emilia Approach – Advanced Reflections*, 2nd edn. Stamford, CT: Ablex, pp. 49–97.

Maslow, A. (1954) *Motivation and Personality*, 2nd edn. New York: Harper & Row.

New Zealand Ministry of Education (1996) *Te Whāriki*. Wellington, NZ: Learning Media.

Mooney, C.G. (2000) *Theories of Childhood: An Introduction to Dewey, Montessori, Erikson, Piaget and Vygotsky*. St Paul, MN: Redleaf Press.

Petrie, P. (2011) *Communication Skills for Working with Children and Young People: Introducing Social Pedagogy*, 3rd edn. London: Jessica Kingsley.

Podmore, V., May, H. and Carr, M. (2001) The 'child's questions': programme evaluation with *Te Whāriki* using 'teaching stories'. *Early Childhood Folio* 5: 6–9.

Rinaldi, C. (2006) *In Dialogue With Reggio Emilia; Listening Researching and Learning*. Hove, UK: Routledge.

Roberts, R. (2010). *Well-Being From Birth*. London: Sage.

Robins G. (2012) *Praise, Motivation and the Child*. London: Routledge.

Rogoff, B. (1990) *Apprenticeship in Thinking: Cognitive Development in Social Context*. New York: Oxford University Press.

Skinner, B.F. (1968) *The Technology of Teaching*. New York: Prentice-Hall.

Smyth, D. (2013) *Person-Centred Therapy With Children and Young People*. London: Sage.

Sylva, K., Melhuish, E., Sammons, P., Siraj- Blatchford, I. and Taggart, B. (2004) *Effective Provision of Pre-School Education (EPPE) Project: Final Report – A Longitudinal Study*. Nottingham: Department for Education and Skills Publications.

Vygotsky, L.S. (1962) *Thought and Language*. Cambridge, MA: MIT Press.

White, J. (2002) *The Child's Mind*. London: Routledge.

Winnicott, D.W. (1965) *The Maturation Process and the Facilitating Environment*. London: Karnac.

Woods, A. (ed.) (2013) *Child-Initiated Play and Learning: Planning for Possibilities in the Early Years*. London: Routledge.

3

Creating effective learning possibilities for all children

Val Hall

Effective teaching for children with SEN shares most of the characteristics of effective learning for all children. But as schools become more inclusive, teachers must be able to respond to a wider range of needs in the classroom.

(Department for Education and Skills, 2004: 55)

As we have seen, one child's well-being will always be based on the individual context of, for and with the child. The way a child thinks and learns is as unique to them as they themselves are unique. In Chapter 5, Gripton is keen to tell us that, when we search for evidence of learning characteristics in all children, regardless of their age and ability, then we are more likely to find what we are searching for. It is important to recognise when we label children, and, although labelling can be beneficial, it can also be linked to 'premature assumptions' about children's learning (Jones, 2004: 24). The label can serve to be the benchmark for what we feel the child can achieve and, therefore, what opportunities may be beneficial to them, thus defining what we search for. If we really feel a child can only achieve a specific target, or that they struggle to learn in a particular way, then we may limit their access to learning. Our thoughts about children influence how we might act towards them. Archetypal methods of observing and recording the characteristics of effective learning in mainstream education can be applicable to children with special educational needs (SEN) (The Scottish Office Education Department, 1994). The European Agency for Special Needs and Inclusive Education (2009: 5) explains that, 'all children have needs'; however, it continues to say, 'some children have special needs'. By resisting a deficit model, it can help us to uncover children's distinctive learning. If we accept that all children are unique, and that settings are becomingly increasingly diverse, then it is also increasingly important to find methods of assessment and observation that function for all children. Moran (in Woods, 2013) explores children's voice, explaining that children who know they are valued feel a sense of belonging. In Reggio Emilia, children are considered to have 'special rights', and this notion of rights is one that includes all (Edwards *et al.*, 2012: 189).

Inclusive learning can be, for some, a 'fundamental shift in attitudes and thinking' (Call and Featherstone, 2010: 39). Thinking in positive terms about what children can do, seeing 'who you are' rather than seeing 'how I can fix you' can help to increase participation and engagement (Macintyre, 2010: 13). Children may have singular ways of thinking and engaging with learning. They may learn at different rates and be motivated by unusual or extraordinary things. When 'people are accepted for who they are', we actively include everyone (Ainscow *et al.*, 2006: 24). An affirmative approach is essential, and Rose and Howley (2007: 13) say, 'it is up to all teachers to begin with an expectation that pupils will learn rather than to make the assumption that they will fail'.

Characteristics of the effective learner: when we celebrate difference

Knowing *how* children learn can help us to build on our understanding of *what* they should learn. The range of diversity in some settings may mean that particular children do not follow 'typical' patterns of child development. The earlier differences significantly impacting on learning are recognised, the earlier appropriate interventions can be introduced, with the specific purpose of meeting need (Tassoni, 2003). Trying to celebrate difference can be problematic. We are often good at integration, whether it be locational, social or functional. More challenging is the notion of inclusion. The language we use is important, as it can dictate our state of mind and, as a result, our feelings as to what is and should be possible. Inclusion, unlike integration, is not static; it is an ongoing process. The language of inclusion helps us to feel that children can and will achieve. It is important for us to foster attitudes to difference that 'embrace not ignore', and this will be key in realistically capturing where children are now and how we can move them forwards (Edwards *et al.*, 2012: 189). Helping children to make progress is easier if we have an understanding of the child's individual 'learning style characteristics', and knowing these should help us to uncover the most appropriate strategies that lead to 'effective learning performance' (Tilstone *et al.*, 2003: 130).

It can be difficult to know if we are getting it right, and at times our confidence can be shaken when we encounter children who test our skills. In the same way as we want to encourage and support children to 'have a go', we should also be brave enough to innovate and try something new.

Encounter: the PE lesson

A TA talks about a boy with attention learning hyperactivity disorder, who struggles to join in with PE. As a result, adults find it difficult to observe his skill level.

> I didn't think he would join in, PE is always so difficult for him, but I thought, 'let's have a go'. He ran around, joined in and managed to take turns with the others and with adult help stayed in his team. He was good at running and managed to throw the bean-bag in the hoop.

Children's skills are impacted by the way in which they learn. Where their skills are limited, this can have a powerful influence on the way in which they view the world. With regard to 'children who experience learning difficulties', Garner (2009: 111) explains they may already have 'a relatively limited repertoire of social skills, and find it difficult to make sense of, and interact with, the world around them'. When trying to create effective learning possibilities for all children, ensuring we make 'exclusion visible' helps us to look more realistically at how we might overcome specific barriers to learning (Jones, 2004: 15). Even if we have high expectations of children, it is also important to be 'sensitive to the subtle ways in which low expectations can be conveyed' (Cole, 2008: 3). There is often a clear link between our views of children and potential learning outcomes.

One way we might create an effective learning environment is to personalise children's learning. Personalised learning and inclusive practice are complementary. Bespoke learning requires thought and organisation if it is to help all children to achieve (Cheminais, 2010). Many teachers differentiate, but to truly personalise learning might take a fundamental shift in understanding about the way in which children think. Where children have a singular world-view, then the way in which they interpret experiences will also be distinct. Classes that embed the concept of individualised learning as part of their good practice, rather than seeing it as exclusive to the child, are better equipped to provide effective teaching (Cornwall and Tod, 1998, in Gibson and Blandford, 2005).

Personalised learning is not just about our knowledge of a child's learning style, but also about our overall knowledge of the child. Having a context for a child's preferred style of learning is essential if we are to help them succeed. Knowing that a child is, for example, an auditory learner is only part of the story. When children have been traumatised, it can mean they adapt from a natural visual preference to an auditory stimulus as a protective mechanism, where waiting for a visual confirmation could be hazardous. How a child's cultural background, or the way in which they communicate, impacts on them can dictate the way in which they currently learn. Layering quality experience upon experience supports the child's willingness to learn. We need to be aware how children will play and explore, create and think, as well as be active in their learning. Where children are not learning at the same rate or in the same way as their peers, it is useful to know if this will always be the way they learn and, therefore, become a means to develop key teaching strategies, or if the way in which they learn may change over time, as they learn new skills and are exposed to countless new experiences. As some children may not only plateau but regress in their development, it is also important to remember that, for those with the most profound difficulties, 'experiences are as important as attainment' (McKewon, 2004: 37). When we value children who have additional needs, we feel they are realistically able to make a contribution. Reciprocally, we need to help children to value themselves. In Chapter 2, Wardle and Vesty highlight the importance of children's well-being and its impact on learning. Helping children to celebrate their own difference and understand their place in the world can build resilience, stimulate their willingness to learn and motivate them to try new things. Children who feel valued and have self-worth are more likely to enjoy and engage in learning (Boxall and Lucas, 2010).

Characteristics of effective schooling: when we learn together

'Relationships' and 'interactions between people' are an essential part of education (Jones, 2004: 15). Creating mutually supportive relationships can help to make access to learning easier, particularly for the very young. As we have already noted, nurturing relationships help children to learn best, developing their resilience and engendering a sense of persistence when faced with difficulties. When children feel connected to learning, they are more able to self-motivate and engage with the learning process. Adults can provide a constant in a child's life, especially when what a child is learning and how they learn continue to change and evolve. Adults can support children in their learning, providing them with situations that are both real and imaginary. When we link these to children's interests, it is more likely that the children will be motivated, and learning will be successful. For some children, interests can become obsessions. When children become engrossed, we need to be able to see the difference between deep-level learning and pure absorption. Understanding the difference can help us learn alongside the child, to develop and extend their interests or, in the case of fascinations, to know how to provide an array of experiences based on a single obsessive curiosity.

Encounter: Matthew's love of trains

Matthew liked trains, all kinds of trains. His parents had taken him on trains, and he constantly watched train videos, both real and imaginary. Matthew could repeat back entire scripts from *Thomas the Tank Engine* videos and collected all of the toys.

Teaching Matthew could be challenging. We initially 'bought in' to his love of trains. We shared in his play with the train track; we completed jigsaws of trains and coloured endless train pictures. We painted trains with finger paints, brushes and sponges. In sand, we drew trains and wrote 'train' underneath. We played trains and chuffed around the room.

Slowly, we introduced a 'first and then', the 'first' being something Matthew had not tried, and the 'then' being a train activity he loved. Gradually, very gradually, we were able to extend his learning to the point where he would tackle new activities and collect train stickers to earn a 'train' reward.

In this encounter, it is possible to see how Matthew is an active learner, as he is able to focus on self-initiated activities for long periods of time. His obsession means that he is rarely distracted; it would be easy to see this in positive terms, but it does mean that Matthew struggles to progress his own learning. Matthew does need supportive adults to help him to apply the same amount of focus and concentration to new and different activities. Matthew would be less willing to have a go at new things without the support of the familiar. Using activities children love as motivators can be highly successful in extending and developing their play. Skilled adults helped Matthew to grow in confidence to explore the unknown, with the understanding and support of the known.

Building reciprocal relationships can present its own challenges. Environments that foster learning can rely on adults who are confident and knowledgeable enough to allow children independence and yet offer reassuring guidance. It is possible for adults to act as 'play partners' and 'act under the direction of the child' (Langston and Doherty, 2012: 171); however, the authors are keen to point out that, 'playful teaching involves practitioners in knowing when and if to intervene in children's play episodes'.

Knowing how to learn alongside children can rely on children telling us. When children are involved in their own learning and they feel they are being listened to, it can have a powerful impact. Seeking children's views about what they like to learn, and how, helps us to plan and promote learning. Even for children with the most profound disabilities, it is possible to gain their opinions. Mercieca (2013: 6) describes children with profound and multiple learning difficulties as 'agents', in that they encourage adults to think creatively about ways in which to capture their voice and opinions. This process helps us to focus our attention and thoughts about the nature of learning.

Encounter: Rachel tells it like it is!

Rachel has social, emotional and behavioural difficulties; she is in Year 5 and is always happy to chat and tell visiting adults about her learning:

> I don't like to learn. I like to dance and I like art, I love my art box. I don't like learning, my mum says we have to learn but I don't know why we come to school. I am not sure what I want to do when I grow up. I might like to design clothes, you know drawing and painting. I don't like teachers, they always shout and say, 'do this, do this.' I like it when Mrs James sits with me, she helps me learn, but sometimes she has to go and work with the other kids, I don't like that, she is supposed to be there for me. When she has to go and work with the others I sit under the desk or run out of the class. I can't do it on my own. I don't really get on well with the other girls, they talk about me and they don't really like to play with me. I don't like to do group work, I like to work with Mrs James.

Here, it is clear that Rachel has low self-esteem, and her experiences of learning have been negative. She does see Mrs James as a supportive influence, and, when she works with Rachel, she is more able to engage her in learning. Rachel's love of art and music is also regularly used as a reward for trying new things. Rachel does have clear ideas and makes choices about her learning; she is able to talk about how she learns, even though it may be in very simplistic terms. Rachel does struggle to be an independent active learner and does not appear to enjoy learning, lacking concentration and giving up easily. Knowing this about Rachel means that adults who support her provide small challenges and big rewards, celebrating every positive attempt.

Characteristics of effective learning environments: when we grow from the child

Featherstone (2013: 6) is keen to point out that experiences should be initiated by the child, that they should be the originators, and cautions adults not to adhere too rigidly to materials that provide a 'to-do list'. Creating opportunities for play may sound as though it conflicts with spontaneous play, but the two are not necessarily in opposition. Cultivating environments that excite and inspire children to play are essential. Equipment and toys that children would not otherwise have had access to, and the chance to make friends and play with others, are critical to development. Widening the scope of children's learning and their social network provides them with exciting experiences and the prospect of playing and having fun. Reflective practitioners are able to respond quickly to the spontaneous play of children. Skilful adults are able to balance the support they give to children, when it is needed, and value the opportunity to stand back and observe, helping them also to build their profile of knowledge about children.

Ainscow *et al.* (2006: 25) highlight that, when attempting to structure effective, inclusive learning environments, it is important to account for the 'cultures, policies and practices in schools so that they respond to the diversity of students in their locality'. Responding to local, individual need helps to create a thoroughly bespoke environment. Adults need to be 'alert to the general diversity of children's interests, needs and inclinations' (Standards and Testing Agency, 2013: 17). Learning cultures are as unique as the children within them, and it is important to set realistic learning targets for all children. Attending to specific needs means being attuned to the environment outside the setting and the way it impacts within the setting. At times, the community of the school presents its own special challenges, some overt, and others subtle.

Encounter: listening to Cyrek

Cyrek is a 4-year-old Polish boy. His teachers acknowledge that English is an additional language (EAL). There are other Polish-speakers in school, but not in Cyrek's class.

Observation

Cyrek is playing in a converted shed outside on the playground. It resembles a home corner, and there is a bed and also some chairs, tables and toys that make it appear familiar. The other children are busy being family members and assigning themselves typical jobs. They move around the space and interact with one another. Cyrek lies on the bed and repeatedly makes crying noises; he not only appears babyish in his role-play, but his overall demeanour is also young in comparison with his peers.

At times, Cyrek speaks, but the other children interpret this as 'baby-talk'. A sensitive adult watching the play offers support: 'juice, I want juice!' The adult pretends to cry and reaches out her hand. Cyrek watches and, after a few minutes, copies the adult's play. Immediately, the other children respond, bringing over a bottle: 'Here Cyrek, have your juice. Biscuit, do you want a biscuit?', to which Cyrek replies, 'Biscuit!' and holds out his hand.

In other environments, this encounter would be different. In his class environment, the lack of other Polish-speaking children means that his EAL has a significant impact on his learning and play. Sensitive modelling by adults and the gentle support from his peers help Cyrek to learn. Adults were also able to put this play into perspective when they later spoke to a Polish TA within the school, who explained that, culturally, Polish children may have extended childhoods, where they assume a learned-helplessness for longer.

Where children have a range of needs, it can be important to ensure they have full access to learning. Farrell (2003: 48) talks in terms of 'equivalent experience' for children with additional needs. Children should 'experience a sense of achievement in order to preserve their self-esteem' (Glazzard *et al.*, 2010: 169). Knowing that there are different ways of learning is important. If children know that they are valued, however they learn, then they have a healthier sense of self-worth.

Growing from the child is particularly important, as they find out about the world through exploratory play. Children play with what they know first and then, with confidence, begin to stretch and challenge themselves, exploring beyond the familiar. Children with additional needs may spend longer in one stage and need extra help to stretch and challenge themselves. 'Recognising the small steps which children make' is essential for children with additional needs and to 'understand that it may take some children longer to achieve specific milestones' (Glazzard *et al.*, 2010: 169). There is a clear correlation between involvement and deep-level learning. If children are happy in their learning, it enables them to be independent future learners. To be able to grow from the child, it is important to find suitable methods to capture success; however, 'we need to be mindful of any summative checks that reduce children's wonderful achievements to something small and ticked' (Brown, in Woods, 2013: 100).

Encounter: tell me how?

A newly qualified teacher (NQT) talks about her experiences and explains:

> I'm not sure how I assess him, am I getting it right? Can you tell me what I should be looking at? He is so different to the other children that I am never sure what I should be teaching him or how. He is a lovely boy and I just want to do my best for him.

This is not just typical of NQTs but is a challenge that faces many adults who try to integrate the needs of distinctive and different children with children who perform typically. Often, observation is our best tool. It provides us with evidence and gives us opportunity to reflect and, hopefully, if we are skilled or just lucky, insight. Matching the best approach to each child may mean using more than one approach to gain different perspectives and then using these to gain a holistic knowledge. Talking to parents and carers is crucial in building an accurate picture of the child's needs; this can also add unique information about likes and dislikes, as well as indicate strengths we do not always know a child has. Within settings, knowledge and use of individual techniques can be beneficial to help us truly grow from the child. Learning stories enable practitioners to capture positive events and experiences, and this 'avoids concentration on deficit models of children's development and learning as the learning story seeks to understand what a child *can do'*. Coates and Thompson (2013: 119) continue to say they are a 'positive affirmation' and they help to support an affirmative ethos.

Encounter: Archie and the water

As a visiting specialist teacher, it is important to work alongside adults to help them see the positive aspects of children. Focus on finding ways to manage their challenges is usually the initial topic of conversation. Archie has a diagnosis of Autistic Spectrum Disorder. His teachers often describe him as difficult to engage, especially in activities that are not of his choosing. Adults also say he has limited concentration and can be easily distracted. During visits, it is understandable that adults often begin conversations by saying what Archie 'can't do' or the problems they have faced managing and teaching him.

Today, I was able to observe Archie outside playing, supported by his TA (who also took photographs of him playing).

Archie is playing alongside four children from his class. They are outside on the playground and have access to a range of plastic washing-up bottles filled with water.

Archie appears to be making random shapes on the playground by squirting the liquid from his bottle. From time to time, his TA comments on what he is doing, 'Look Archie, a circle'. Archie pauses to look at his work and then continues to squirt water in ever increasing circles. Accidentally, he squirts water over the foot of another child, who jumps back shouting 'ooooh!' Archie looks up and laughs, he squirts again, this time intentionally and the children engage in a water fight, but only aiming the water at each other's toes.

Archie goes back to drawing his circles and this time says 'circle'. The TA draws attention to another child who is writing their name with the water on the playground. Archie stops squirting and goes over to look; he mouths the name spelled on the playground and uses the water bottle to write his own, saying it aloud. Archie smiles.

Today, it is easier to talk to adults and say that Archie is capable of sustained shared play and he can be encouraged to have a go and engage in learning not of his own choosing. Archie also showed enjoyment finding out and experimenting with the water. Significantly, his positive interactions with other children should not be underestimated. The photographs of Archie squirting water and smiling with his friends will be a powerful representation and provide key evidence to encourage similar experiences.

Fundamental to good learning stories is that they should see the child as a competent learner (Carr and Lee, 2012). They should reflect the child in a positive light and ultimately add to our knowledge of the child; from this encounter, the learning story helped adults to provide similar experiences and to identify characteristics of Archie's learning that they might not have been able to identify through traditional assessments.

Timed observations are also a useful device to highlight children's learning, described by Green (2002: 413) as 'a method used to observe a child at regular intervals throughout a planned period of time'.

According to Brodie (2013: 62), time sampling can show the highest level of involvement by showing moments of *deep interest*; however, these may only be snapshots, and, to talk in terms of embedded learning, repeated observations over time would be necessary. They can identify 'cause for concern' (Green, 2002: 413), and these can be helpful for identifying interventions. Time sampling in isolation may only provide a superficial knowledge of the child and can be at its best when linked to other strategies, for instance referencing the context, the environment of learning, or by assessing the outcome of learning: for example, did the child complete the task set during the observation to an acceptable level?

Encounter: Ahmed and the story – time sampling

Ahmed is in Year 1 and he is often described by staff as a 'bouncy' child. They report that he finds it difficult to access story sessions on the carpet the same as his peers. He often gets up and wanders around, fiddling with equipment and talking over his teacher as she reads aloud. Staff say they are unsure if he learns 'anything' at story time. A 1-minute-interval, time-sampled observation was completed. This highlighted that he does appear to spend more time 'on task' than previously thought.

The time sampling itself needed to be placed into a context of what learning Ahmed had made. Following the observation, an adult sat with Ahmed with a copy of the book. Although a little chaotic in his thoughts and at times showing some muddled recall, it was clear he had picked up a range of information and could repeat back the thread of the story and name key characters.

Ahmed's frenzied movement in the class focused adult attention; at times, the disruption this caused to the rest of the class and the adults' attempts to manage this successfully masked what Ahmed might actually be learning.

Once the results of the observations and the individual work with Ahmed had been reported back to staff, they were able to say:

> I had thought that he didn't really join in with the class activities, most of his time he seems to be wandering around the room or talking. Looking at the timed observation of him, I can see he spends more time learning than I had thought.

Perhaps the most common form of observation that helps support our ability to grow from the child and extend our knowledge is narrative observation. Narrative observation uses everyday language to record 'what the participant says or does' (Mukherji and Albon, 2010: 108).

Although subjective, observations can present a clear picture of each child. They can help practitioners to identify areas of concern and points for action. Even where observations clearly depict children engaged in less than appropriate behaviour, when shared with parents, they often agree that that is an accurate picture of their child.

Truthful representations, in everyday language, can serve as a starting point in a process to meet need precisely.

Encounter: Owen rocks!

Owen is in Year 3 and he has been identified as having social, emotional and behavioural difficulties. He frequently disrupts his own learning and that of his class. A narrative observation was completed and shared with staff and parents.

Owen is in class; there are twenty-eight other children and his class teacher. Children are sitting on group tables, and Owen is on a table with five other children. Children are completing target sheets about their learning. Other children have been able to explain to the observer what they are working on and have repeatedly pointed out to Owen that there is 'someone at the back of the class watching us'.

Owen rocks on his chair; at first, he appears distracted, and then his rocking increases. As he leans back, it is easier to reach a boy sitting on another table. He taps at the boy's head and pokes him in the back with a pencil. The boy ignores him. Owen repeats the actions, rocking, tapping and poking. When the boy reacts and tells him to 'Get lost!', Owen stops rocking and begins to write. Other children on Owen's table appear to be helping him with his writing. Owen looks up and appears to be looking at the display board; he then looks across the room, checking in to see what his teacher is doing. She smiles and points at the table, indicating to him to continue with his work. Owen writes on his paper and then begins to rock slowly on his chair. He rocks more frenetically and then prods the same boy with a pencil.

The narrative observation in this encounter does depict Owen in a negative light. His current behaviour does impact on his own learning and that of others. However, the narrative observation was able to start a dialogue between parents and school. Seating arrangements for Owen were also considered, and importantly sensory breaks were included, so that Owen had the opportunity to move around at frequent intervals to help support short-focused bursts of learning.

For some children, their barriers to learning may not be so obvious. Tracking individual children may help to uncover the personal issues they have. Following a child around their environment can highlight, not only how they move around the space, but also how they might access resources. Tracking can tell us how they interact with others as part of their learning and where children are reliant on adults to engineer learning situations, for instance wheel-chair users pushed by adults. This can also show us ways we might provide opportunities to develop and promote learning. Recording routes that are taken and activities the child is able to physically access can help us to ask ourselves if we need to physically redesign the environment, improving layouts or investing in new equipment so that it is user-friendly. Changing spaces to provide a flexible enough environment so that it co-evolves with the needs of the child is crucial. Physical barriers can not only impact on opportunities, but also add to 'negative labelling' (Jones, 2004: 16). Children's responses may also show us who they are best paired with to encourage positive learning outcomes, selecting those children who are able to bring out the best in others. Tracking can also show us what children avoid. Knowing what they dislike can be as important as knowing what they like.

The most powerful means of learning about all children is to ask them. Chats, and even formalised interviews, with children can help us to uncover what they feel. Knowing what children want and feel helps to complete the jigsaw of what helps them to be an effective learner. Where children are confident learners, they are more able to make decisions for their own learning, and when they are capable of making simple choices, they are more likely to be able to progress and make bigger, more complex choices.

Encounter: singing and dancing

Prior to a small group targeted to help children with social interaction and friendship issues, a 'chat' was conducted with the child participants. Although they all had different views about friendship and were different learners, they had one thing in common, they liked to sing and dance.

In group sessions, all of the children were reluctant to discuss and talk openly about their problems, but, when familiar music was played and the children began to dance, they found themselves talking frankly and more openly than when they were faced with direct questioning.

Principles for effective learning need to account for children's feelings of safety and security. Learning environments can significantly impact on children's learning (Gargiulo and Kilgo, 2011). It is important that educational settings focus on the relationship dimension and are not 'simply buildings or curriculum plans' (Jones, 2004: 15). Andrews (2012: 61) cautions us not to bring 'baggage' to our observations; often, the 'adults are immigrants entering a child's culture'. It is a skill to shed our preconceptions and use experiences to consider fresh approaches.

Characteristics of effective adults: when teaching takes a different approach

When assessing if a child has SEN, one of the judgements should be on the 'child's learning characteristics' (Farrell, 2004: 20). For children with disabilities, holistic approaches may be best, as children's disabilities rarely impact solely on one single area. Adults need to acknowledge and be 'fully committed to the view that all their pupils and students are capable of learning' (The Scottish Office Education Department, 1994: 13).

> Many practitioners are either reluctant or feel they do not have the skills to identify any additional needs of children in their care. This could be for many reasons including fear of approaching parents, fear of labelling children or fear of getting it wrong.
>
> (Dukes and Smith, 2009: x)

Adults often know their children well, and, although they are not required to diagnose children, they can contribute important information that helps to emphasise key learning needs. An adult's view of the child can impact on what they feel the child is capable of achieving and, as a result, the style of learning and the assessment that may be required (Glazzard *et al.*, 2010). Matching teaching and learning creates effective learning environments. Access to engaging curricula is essential, even if it is difficult to provide authentic, rather than contrived, situations.

Adults who respond well to children with special needs are those who are flexible and display for themselves key learning characteristics. Often, they are skilled at finding out what a child likes and dislikes. They know how to play with children and what will motivate children to join in and have a go. Their support of children during active learning is critical, and they maximise learning opportunities, knowing when to step in and when to step back. Not only do they enjoy seeing children learn, they enjoy learning from the child and they encourage children to be creative and think for themselves. There is the potential for radical change when adults encourage children to 'generate their own ideas' (Hutchin, 2013: 16).

Levels of arousal and stimulation for children with diverse needs can be crucial factors in helping to motivate them. Being 'ready, willing and able' forms an essential part of dispositions towards learning (Carr, 2001: 21). Searching for optimum levels to support children may mean indulging in creative, 'out-of-the-box' thinking. Inspired adults help children to find their own curious new ways of thinking by empowering children to think for themselves; 'if we take control of it, it is no longer the child's agenda and is unlikely to bring about learning' (Hutchin, 2013: 12). Where children feel in control of their learning and consider they have a voice, then learning outcomes are improved. This is also true of children with the most profound and multiple learning difficulties: having 'opportunity to take control' is essential (Tilstone *et al.*, 2003: 149).

The willingness and skill of supportive adults are essential components when helping children to 'extend and consolidate' learning (Fisher, 2013: 57). Knowing not only what to observe, but also how, is key to assessment. For children with additional needs, it is important that they should not be thought of as separate, but they may need professionals to pick from an array of assessment techniques ones that are best suited and well matched to individual needs. Professionals will need to understand how to reconcile the fact that children with additional needs are not homogeneous with an educational system that assesses at set points in time, regardless of age, maturity or rates of development. Enjoying achieving is when we take pride in ourselves, rather than feeling the need to measure ourselves against what others may see. This is true, not only of children, but also of the adults who support them. Braveness based on knowledge can be inspirational.

Encounter: talking to early years specialist teachers

Question
'Tell me about the challenges of recording the characteristics of effective learning for children with additional needs.'

Amalgamated response
The hardest thing is their spiky development, one day they can do something and the next they can't. It can be difficult to help teachers to know how to record that. Sometimes children have gaps in their learning and do not always build on one skill before leaping ahead with something else. They can have strengths in odd areas, particularly if they have an interest in something and that motivates them to learn one specific thing. The opposite can also be true, they can have a reluctance to learn something and even though it appears they have the skills, they do not always demonstrate they can do it. Teachers then struggle to observe it often enough to be able to evidence it. Some children appear to rely heavily on the support of an adult and this can also influence how others see the child, it is not always clear if they would have done something instinctively had the adult not initiated it first.

The fact is that children may be able to perform and achieve a task one day, and then it can be many days or weeks before this achievement is observed again. They may also skip stages, or need to take a step back before they can move forwards. Some children also regress. This can be difficult to record on progress sheets that record a smooth transition from one level of success to another. Accepting that some children may make small steps and that progress for other children may be limited is important. Adults are unable to watch or document every moment within a child's day, and it is natural to expect that some achievements may be missed. It is also important to remember the 'quiet' child, who may often go unnoticed, or, for that matter, the child we know is reaching milestones and achieving beyond expectations but who is not demanding of our attention, as they too may be overlooked. Experience is as important as outcome, and quality experiences are, therefore, vital. Having fun along the way can help to motivate and engage reluctant learners. Adults who have developed good relationships with children can encourage them to participate in unexpected or extraordinary activities. Children are better able to select and choose activities for themselves if they have awareness and familiarity. They are able to link experiences to feelings, and this can help them to make judgements. Supportive adults may need to act as advocates for children who find it difficult to make their opinions known. Having a clear understanding of the child's preferences is key, if experiences are to be meaningful to the child and not just the 'easy' option for the adult. The key to successful progress, even for those with the 'most severe and complex needs' in 'all types of settings' is 'high quality specialist teachers and commitment by leaders to make opportunities' (Ofsted, 2006, in National College for School Leadership, 2009: 6). Being able to capture and reflect magic moments, 'where something entirely new and different seems to be coming about' (Olsson, 2009: 63) provides us with the potential to create effective learning possibilities for all children, and this will be further examined in Moran's chapter (Chapter 8).

When assessing characteristics of effective learning, where there is a clear focus on process rather than merely outcome, it is more likely to be successful. This philosophy is especially true for children with additional needs. Their journey may be slower, distinctive and, yes, even special, but the process is most definitely important and relies on key adults who are able to adopt a positive perspective and look for things a child 'can do'. High-quality, supportive adults see children as competent learners playing, exploring and thinking in extraordinary ways.

Provocations

- What do you think of as 'celebrating' children? Can you think of how you might celebrate the learning characteristics of all children in your setting?

- Think of a time recently when you have been able to share the success of a child others often see of as challenging; did it help to change their views?

- Have you considered doing a physical audit of your setting, possibly tracking one child to see how they access the space, interact with others and maximise their learning? Think how you might use your findings to adapt and change your setting.

- What are the possibilities in your setting to incorporate different styles of observation to learn more about your children? Have a go at a narrative observation, relying on having an affirmative view of the child.

- Can you identify a child in your setting who finds it difficult to make themselves heard? Think of ways you can get to know that child, so you can advocate for them.

- Think of possibilities that will create secure environments where children feel safe and where they feel their voice is being listened to. How will this affect the way in which these children are then able to learn and access the curriculum?

References

Ainscow, M., Booth, T., Dyson, A., Farrell, P., Frankham, J., Gallannaugh, F., Howes, A. and Smith, R. (2006) *Improving Schools, Developing Inclusion*. Abingdon, UK: Routledge.

Andrews, M. (2012) *Exploring Play for Early Childhood Studies*. London: Sage.

Boxall, M. and Lucas, S. (2010) *Nurture Groups in School Principles and Practice*, 2nd edn. London: Sage.

Brodie, K. (2013) *Observation, Assessment and Planning in the Early Years: Bringing it All Together*. Maidenhead, UK: McGraw-Hill.

Call, N. and Featherstone, S. (2010) *The Thinking Child: Brain-Based Learning for the Early Years Foundation Stage*. London: Continuum International.

Carr, M. (2001) *Assessment in Early Childhood Settings: Learning Stories*. London: Sage.

Carr, M. and Lee, W. (2012) *Learning Stories: Constructing Learner Identity in Early Education*. London: Sage.

Cheminais, R. (2010) *Handbook for New SENCOs*. London: Sage.

Coates, D. and Thompson, W. (2013) Using learning stories in the Early Years Foundation Stage. In Palaioulogou, I. (ed.) *The Early Years Foundation Stage Theory and Practice*. London: Sage, pp. 118–31.

Cole, R.W. (ed.) (2008) *Educating Everybody's Children: Diverse Teaching Strategies for Diverse Learners*, 2nd edn. Alexandria, VA: Association for Supervision and Curriculum Development.

Department for Education and Skills (2004) *Removing Barriers to Achievement: The Government's Strategy for SEN*. Nottingham, UK: Department for Education and Skills.

Dukes, C. and Smith, M. (2009) *Recognising and Planning for Special Needs in the Early Years*. London: Sage.

Edwards, C., Gandini, L. and Forman, G. (eds) (2012) *The Hundred Languages of Children: The Reggio Emilia Experience in Transformation*. Santa Barbara, CA: Praeger.

European Agency for Special Needs and Inclusive Education (2009) *Assessment for Learning and Pupils with Special Educational Needs*. Available online at: www.european-agency.org (accessed 1 May 2014).

Farrell, M. (2003) *Understanding Special Educational Needs: A Guide for Student Teachers*. London: Routledge Falmer.

Farrell, M. (2004) *Inclusion at the Crossroads: Special Education – Concepts and Values*. London: David Fulton.

Featherstone, S. (2013) *Supporting Child-Initiated Learning: Like Bees, Not Butterflies*. London: Bloomsbury.

Fisher, J. (2013) *Starting From the Child*. Maidenhead, UK: McGraw-Hill.

Gargiulo, R.M. and Kilgo, J.L. (2011) *An Introduction to Young Children with Special Needs Birth Through Age Eight*. Belmont, CA: Cengage.

Garner, P. (2009) *Special Educational Needs: The Key Concepts*. Abingdon, UK: Routledge.

Gibson, S. and Blatchford, S. (2005) *Managing Special Educational Needs: A Practical Guide for Primary and Secondary Schools*. London: Sage.

Glazzard, J., Chadwick, D., Webster, A. and Percival, J. (2010) *Assessment for Learning in the Early Years Foundation Stage*. London: Sage.

Green, S. (2002) *BTEC National Early Years*. Cheltenham, UK: Nelson Thornes.

Hutchin, V. (2013) *Effective Practice in the Early Years Foundation Stage: An Essential Guide*. Maidenhead, UK: McGraw-Hill.

Jones, C. (2004) *Supporting Inclusion in the Early Years*. Maidenhead, UK: McGraw-Hill.

Langston, A. and Doherty, J. (2012) *Thinking, Reflecting and Doing! The Revised EYFS in Practice*. London: Featherstone Education.

Macintyre, C. (2010) *Play for Children With Special Needs: Supporting Children With Learning Differences, 3–9*, 2nd edn. Abingdon, UK: Routledge.

McKewon, S. (2004) *Meeting Special Needs in the Curriculum: Modern Foreign Languages*. London: David Fulton.

Mercieca, D.P. (2013) *Living Otherwise: Students With Profound and Multiple Learning Disabilities as Agents in Educational Contexts*. Rotterdam, The Netherlands: Sense.

Mukherji, P. and Albon, D. (2010) *Research Methods in Early Childhood: An Introductory Guide*. London: Sage.

National College for School Leadership (NCSL) (2009) *Achievement for All: Characteristics of Effective Inclusive Leadership – a Discussion Document*. Nottingham, UK: NCSL.

Olsson, L.M. (2009) *Experimentation in Young Children's Learning: Deleuze and Guatarri in Early Childhood Education*. Abingdon, UK: Routledge.

Rose, R. and Howley, M. (2007) *The Practical Guide To Special Educational Needs in the Primary Classroom*. London: Sage.

The Scottish Office Education Department (1994) *Effective Provision for Special Educational Needs* Edinburgh: The Scottish Office Education Department.

Standards and Testing Agency (2013) *National Curriculum Assessments Early Years Foundation Stage Profile Handbook*. Cheshire, UK: Department for Education. Available online at: www.education.gov.uk/eyfsp (accessed 1 May 2014).

Tassoni, P. (2003) *Supporting Special Needs: Understanding Inclusion in the Early Years*. Oxford, UK: Heinnemann.

Tilstone, C., Florian, L. and Rose, R. (eds) (2003) *Promoting Inclusive Practice*, London: Routledge.

Woods, A. (ed.) (2013) *Child-Initiated Play and Learning: Planning for Possibilities in the Early Years*. London: Routledge.

4

Children's engaging interests

Annie Woods

It may be argued that:

> Always and everywhere children take an active role in the construction and acquisition of learning and understanding. So it is that in many situations, especially when one sets up challenges, children show us they know how to walk along the path to understanding. Once children are helped to perceive themselves as authors or inventors, once they are helped to discover the pleasure of inquiry, their motivation and interest explode.
>
> (Malaguzzi, in Edwards *et al.*, 1998: 67)

McEwan, in Chapter 1, has shown us that from being very young babies, children are exploring, transforming, creating, experimenting, playing with and enjoying experiences, relationships and materials. The context of problem solving is also explored by Gripton (Chapter 5), and how we might document these diverse, observed activities will be discussed by Moran (Chapter 8). This chapter considers the playfulness of children's learning and the *disposition* to be ready, willing and able to pursue a project or schema of ideas actively, 'observed to be a sort of "fingering over" of the environment in sensory terms, a questioning of the power of materials as a preliminary to the creation of higher organization of meaning' (Cobb, 1977: 48). I will discuss the notion of dispositions (characteristics of effective learning) and suggest that a child's project or enduring interest, like Piaget's schema, is a necessary developmental drive or enquiry for learning, often repeated, certainly observable and an indication of active internal thought processes.

Transforming ideas

An afternoon encounter in a reception classroom is evidence of *making sense of ideas and materials through active exploration*. Both the following encounters take place at the making table:

Encounter: Tim playing and exploring

On the making table, Tim is puzzling out how to join two elastic bands together. Through trial and error, he winds sticky tape between the two and joins them to a box as a ladder; he then realises it can be used as a catapult. 'They sit here and bounce into the sea [pulls elastic]; there are no sharks . . . as they bouncing into the other boat. Quick. Climb on, quick put the roof on.' The box model flies into the air on to the floor accompanied by a 'brrrrrrrrrrrrr' engine noise.

His active learning is transforming ideas into a unique object.

Encounter: Oliver actively learning

Me: This is beginning to look like something special.
Oliver: It's a transformer. A bumble bee. This is a gun to get the baddies.
Tim: Can I have the masking tape? It's so strong.
Oliver: Stronger than sticky tape.

How do they *know* it is stronger? Through active experiences on the making table, the everyday resources affording the possibility of finding out the appropriate material for the purpose at hand – a strong tape to join two objects. The boys are finding this out through active play. Oliver's 'transformer' is a plastic tray, bottle, fluffy head and pipe-cleaner legs enveloped in masking tape. He draws a face on the transformer. He is then asked by another child to make another. In a fraction of the time carefully taken over the first model (around 40 minutes), he chooses a tray, a bottle and tape, quickly assembling another transformer. His active learning itself is a *transformation* of ideas, materials and emerging skills; Rogoff (1990, in Brooker and Edwards, 2010: 39) 'defines learning as the transformation of participation in cultural activities', with Edwards *et al.* (in Broadhead *et al.*, 2010: 136) reiterating that, 'process over product supports children's learning and knowledge acquisition. Process over product has been emphasised as an important component of learning, suggesting that the act of participation in play is more important than what the play itself generates'. A discussion with the foundation teacher after these encounters reinforced that both Tim and Oliver could be found at the making table most days, refining their design skills and *projecting* both their imaginative and media recollections on to original models. The 'help-yourself' resources supported their 'having an intellectual "can-do" approach, as it were, one which is open to the possibility of ideas "popping into one's head" and being taken seriously, and this approach being brought to a range of situations, repeatedly' (Craft, 2002: 90). The culture of this classroom being one where children could investigate, experiment, find and combine resources, Tim and Oliver were fully participative.

Playfulness

Dewey tells us:

> [So] when children play horse, play store, play house or making calls, they are subordinating the physically present to the ideally signified. In this way, a world of meanings, a store of concepts (so fundamental to all intellectual achievement), is defined and built up. Moreover, not only do meanings thus become familiar acquaintances, but they are organised, arranged in groups, made to cohere in connected ways.
>
> (1910: 161–2)

Further, he argues that, '*Playfulness* is a more important consideration than play. The former is an attitude of mind; the latter is a passing outward manifestation of this attitude' (p. 162). It is in playfulness that we see characteristics of effective learning, children using what they know in their play and achieving what they set out to do.

Encounter: Steve and Simon using what they know in their play

Steve and Simon (twin brothers) transform past experiences into new play actions.
There are a great number of boughs to use in the woods – of different lengths, all transportable by one, or usually two children. I notice that the brothers have begun to lay some boughs out in a grid-like pattern in the clearing. They appear to be working to a definite idea, although there is little shared discussion apart from, 'let's find two longer and a number of shorter pieces to make a ladder'. The grid becomes their aeroplane. They sit on the seat – a thicker piece of bough – and rest a shorter bough across their laps . . . and take off. The short bough is a gear/steering prop. The accompanying noises are of a motor. The noise stops, the prop is lifted and put to one side – rather like a constraining bar on a fairground ride. The brothers climb over (down) the ladder, talking to themselves about climbing down from the plane, and go on their holiday. They return to the plane, take off and repeat the flight play a number of times before finally reaching 'their destination'.

Once again, this encounter takes place and *is observed* where the culture of playfulness is valued, constructed by the children and the adult observer/ participant; outcomes are demonstrated where 'the degrees of freedom allowed to the actors' (Edwards *et al.*, cited in Broadhead *et al.*, 2010: 198) somehow 'flip the curriculum'. Being asked to create a two-dimensional model in the wood clearing would not have been so enriching. We may question whether the boughs being lifted and laid down was purposeful at the start, whether the act of trans- porting the sticks was the initial focus, whether an airplane shape imaginatively revealed itself; suffice to say, once the boys developed a mutual goal – flying to different holiday destinations – the play was novel, exploratory and shared. The boys often transported themselves across the spaces in the woodland environ- ment, creating a framed pretend pond with boughs, tying string to boughs for fishing rods and climbing up trees to lie in the branches. They seemed to have had a close sibling understanding of play ideas; they also lived on a small farm and rode horses, where boughs would be constructed into low jumps. This contextual information helps us to both interpret and identify durable and effective characteristics of learning. Rogoff (1990) claims that:

> Playful exploration among children may be especially important for devel- oping new solutions to a problem, as information obtained by goofing around with the materials may suggest novel, creative solutions to problems down the line. Hence it may be important in studying the character of peer inter- action to use tasks and situations in which peers feel enjoyment and freedom, and to observe long enough to determine the long-range advantages that may come from wandering exploration along the way.
>
> (Rogoff, 1990: 186)

Physical playfulness with materials is a natural part of development, particularly for children, but also for all humans, who *need* to explore materials in order to understand them and use them.

Needham suggests:

> Knowledge it is argued, is not something that exists performed to be discovered, it is rather developed through the evolution of human activity. Humanity has developed both physical tools and mental tools through experience and the desire to achieve certain goals. Knowledge will always be evolving in the light of what we seek to do and will always build upon the cultural practices of the past. We develop through learning to participate in the use of physical tools [for example] (writing materials) and mental tools (language) that are available to us to adapt the environment in which we find ourselves.
>
> (in Waller *et al.*, 2011: 57)

Tim and Oliver, as discussed with the reception teacher, spent much of their current play time on the making table, a table we all recognise as 'flipping the curriculum'; children design, choose, create, narrate and repeat successful joining/fixing activity and enjoy the flexibility of resources and creating something *that stands for something else*. Hakkarainen (1999, cited by Needham, in Waller *et al.*, 2011)

> asserted that the purpose of play from the child's perspective is related to the mastery of tools, with play affording a forum to repeat and try out alternate performances in a relatively low risk and pleasurable physical and social context.
>
> (Waller *et al.*, 2011: 83)

Tim and Oliver were taken seriously by an adult sitting alongside (me), occasionally commenting and adding narrative to their own explanations of what they were doing and why, in what I perceived to be a pleasurable social context *and* within their time frame. I would argue this was more valuable than the two interruptions that also occurred during their play.

Encounter: Charles and the propeller

Charles (TA) to Tim: What are you making? It's not another spaceship?

Tim did not answer.

Charles: What else does the boat need? Does it need propellers?

Tim either chose not to answer, or was too engrossed in his play to respond to these fleeting questions, and Charles passed on to the next set of children. A while later, a second TA came to the same making table, where Oliver and Sophie were deeply involved in their models.

Encounter: Oliver is busy

TA: I need you to come and do a job.
Oliver: I'm busy making something.
TA: You need to come now.

Oliver looked over to me for reassurance (?) that I would look after his model, and he and Sophie followed the TA to an adjacent table for some handwriting practice. (It was towards the end of term; did examples need to be collected?)

Five minutes later, the children returned to the making table, and I noticed that, when Oliver completed his model, he turned it over, found a marker pen and wrote OLIVERS on the back, worthy of note and a photograph, and perhaps a more useful learning story to illustrate a curriculum outcome.

Fortunately, the flow of the modelling activities had sustained their desire to return to their play. This flow framed the time they needed to achieve what they set out to do, and we need to afford this time for the children, as well as facilitate our own ability to observe how deeply they become involved when led by their own decisions and actions. Gripton, in Chapter 5, also considers time as crucial for children to be able to explore alternative answers and solutions. It is useful to return to Cousins' observations, when she talks about 4-year-old Sonnyboy, an intensely curious traveller child:

> As with the child in the story 'The Emperor's New Clothes', Sonnyboy spoke out against the seemingly ridiculous or obvious. Once he had settled into school, he questioned his teacher about those irritating interruptions with 'why'd you interrupt us so?' In particular, he disliked the bell and one playtime when it rang loudly in the corridor, Sonnyboy was heard grumbling. 'That don't make no sense . . . I just got to the interesting bit, I don't care about the time, that's plain stupid . . . *time's as long as it takes* [my italics].
>
> (Cousins, 1999:36)

'Getting to the interesting bit' is surely what we are looking for in the activities we offer, the resources available and the diverse means by which children should be encouraged to think about, plan for and *project* their ideas, within and beyond curriculum areas. Howard suggests:

> There are certain cues that children appear sensitive to when making play judgements. In addition, it appears that practitioners have a certain level of control in terms of the development of this sensitivity. Perceived playfulness is maximised when children are afforded control, when adults engage in all types of activity and when activities are not constrained by where they take place. Essentially, play is maximised when practitioners communicate that it is of equal value to other activities.
>
> (in Broadhead *et al.*, 2010: 156)

Children's projects

The inclusion of areas such as the making table, with a display of various, changing resources, affords children the possibility of active learning and exploration, and recreating images and representations of objects from current and past memory, media or actual experiences. Tolman asks us to:

> Consider a child learning to drive nails with a hammer. Is it merely learning responses? Is it merely learning to adapt to the demands of the wood, the nails, or the hammer? The child *is* learning responses and *is* learning to adapt to demands, but not merely. The hammer, like all objects made by human beings, from the simplest implements to the computer, embodies meaning, the accumulated historical experience of the society into which the child is born, and it is this above all that the child is acquiring. It is the knowledge of making things and of the need to do so, of the utility of wood, of the functions of nails and hammers. The child is appropriating societal experience.
>
> (in Engeström *et al.*, 1999: 74–5)

Tim and Oliver were demonstrating very strong dispositions towards creative and technical activity because of the open-endedness of materials, in the earlier examples, particularly the properties of tape, elastic, the tape cutter and scissors. They had also initiated their own *projects*, thus 'flipping the curriculum' to child-led enquiry and outcomes. Broadhead *et al.* recognise that:

> within the three to five age range, we were finding extensive evidence of metacognitive or self-regulatory behaviours which most frequently occurred during learning activities which were initiated by the children, involved them in working in pairs or small groups, and which entailed extensive collaboration and talk.
>
> (2010: 166)

They also found that practitioners found involving themselves in playful activity with children more difficult than in those activities that were adult directed. It may be argued, therefore, that characteristics of effective learning are present, but more evident and demonstrable in child-led activity.

Debbie Ryder, a colleague and head teacher from New Zealand, had found in Reggio Emilia, in 2003, that, 'the teaching and learning spaces were open and uncluttered with detailed pieces of work being carefully displayed throughout the environment' (unpublished: 1). Responsible for the infants and toddlers in her centre, she worked with a project approach, 'an emergent form of planning strongly influenced by the actions of a child or a group of children' (ibid.: 3) or 'inquiry based learning' (ibid.: 4). Having identified the needs of an individual child and how he preferred to be settled outdoors when his mum left, Debbie introduced more natural resources to the indoor environment.

Encounter: throwing out the plastic

A search in the cupboard found a beautiful variety of stones and shells. These were then added to the everyday items – it was interesting to observe the young children as they encountered the small shells and stones – would they put them in their mouths? It seemed though that the children were far more interested in these natural materials than just wanting to put them in their mouths, they wanted to experience what they felt like, sounded like, etc.

Due to a bad patch in the weather and an ever increasing interest in the shells and stones, we were beginning to bring our outside environment inside for the children to experience and they became a normal part of our inside materials. We were noticing that these natural materials were holding the children's interest where the plastic toys were not. It was at this stage that we decided we wanted natural and everyday materials to be not just a part of the programme, but to be the programme we offered children. After a month of observation, we concluded that we wanted to take all the plastic equipment out of the centre, and would work with natural and suitable wooden materials. At this point, shells and stones were aesthetically displayed, the environment arranged in a wonderfully welcoming way for children and adults alike – more and more children and adults are being drawn to the infant and toddler area.

Outside, we realised that we could no longer just rely on the sandpit, grass and plastic slide to provide stimulating experiences; major physical changes needed to occur if the outside environment would provoke experiences of inquiry to occur in the same way as was now occurring inside.

Across from the pebble pit is an area for exploration and climbing, natural logs, boulders, and tree stumps provide for highly skilled climbing challenges. The bridge serves as an area of transition between the small concrete area for bouncing balls etc. through to the natural environment. A seat has been positioned so that children and adults can share some time together.

The following learning story is just one of many that describe our new environment in action.

It was near the end of the day and a few children came outside with me as I was clearing things away. Dawn and I noticed the way that the environment was offering Keiran a new challenge as he climbed up and over the large log to get into the sandpit. He stayed in the sandpit for an extended period of time as he explored the texture of the sand. As he got up he thought about how he could get out, and it was then that he wandered over to the end where there is a gap between the log and the fence. Then something caught his attention – it was our new sculpture that I had placed outside by the tree. Keiran crawled over to it and stared at it for a short time, not too sure as to what it was – but it certainly caught his attention. He then crawled past the sculpture to settle in his favourite spot – among the pebbles! We played together with the pebbles, lifting them up high and trickling them through our fingers, and listening while they dropped back down again. We repeated this action for a while. He enjoyed the feel of the pebbles under his feet and spent some time kicking his legs back and forth – digging his feet further into the pebbles to 'feel' them even more! As we continued to play together, Keiran began making really loud noises – as if he was calling out, he could hear the older children playing in the over-twos – was he calling out to them? Keiran would look around and then call out again, enjoying using his voice in this new way – I wonder what he was saying?

I wonder if he was relating to his prior experience of our recent trip to the beach with his mum and preschool friends. We know that an effective curriculum is one which links prior 'known' experiences that happen outside the centre, for example, our trip to the beach, with experiences within the centre – shells, pebbles, driftwood. Then Keiran heard a voice he recognised, and as he looked towards the inside he saw his mum – a big smile went on his face as he recognised who it was, and off he went to greet her!

(Ryder, unpublished: 7–12)

Children's play preferences, their enquiries and their explorations can be deeply expressed through relationships with people, places and things – things that are actual objects, or abstract ideas formed through their learning enquiries. The environmental *affordances* of Debbie's centre and the careful research of children's attitudes towards an active exploration of materials combined to support the development of strong and robust characteristics of effective learning and promote children's own projects or learning enquiries. Craft (2002: 44) implies that:

> 'little c creativity' is the notion that it is essentially a practical matter akin to Ryle's . . . 'know-how', in that it is concerned with the skills involved in manoeuvring and operating with concepts, ideas, and the physical and social world.

This 'fingering over' (Cobb, 1977) is suggestive of Piaget's theory of schematic play, and a project or learning enquiry appears to be driven by a desire to make sense of a thing or idea, repeatedly. Rinaldi (in Dahlberg and Moss, 2005: 106–7) considers, 'The word "project" evokes the idea of a dynamic process, an itinerary. It is sensitive to the rhythms of communication and incorporates the significance and timing of children's investigations and research.' Keiran, earlier, returns to his 'favourite' place – the pebble pit. He may be revisiting his beach experience, estimating the weight of the pebbles, using his feet to dig holes, making sounds or investigating gravity, but he is clearly following a line of his own enquiry, and this is similar to Freya's earlier encounter in McEwan's Chapter 1. Hedges (in Broadhead *et al.*, 2010: 30) claims that, 'Funds of knowledge feed forward and feedback into interests at each stage of the continuum. Play is a central way in which children demonstrate, re-visit and extend interests; representing these in all points of the curriculum.' We can also consider:

> When young children play they have an agenda independent of anything we adults might want to do. It is as if they are embarking on a research programme, where they are collecting and analysing data, and constructing and testing their own theories of what life is all about.

(Hughes, 2012: 79)

Active exploration

As we have seen earlier, Tim, Oliver, Steve and Simon were actively demonstrating unique, creative models or representations from materials at hand; Keiran, a very young child, was actively exploring his environment, beginning to make sense of and connect sensory memories and beginning to 'know' the properties of different materials. Cobb (1977: 48) again reminds us that, 'For every child all the world is new, and freshness of sensory experience abounds'. Donaldson also claims that:

> Most of the knowledge that matters to us – the knowledge that constitutes our conception of the world, of other people and of ourselves – is not developed in a passive way. We come to know through processes of active interpretation and integration. We ask questions . . . We have strategies of many kinds of finding out . . . we struggle to make sense.
>
> (1992: 19)

The boys were acquiring information through active exploration initiated by themselves, transforming resources; Rogoff (1990: 186) suggests we might call this 'goofing around', but it is the acquisition and transformation that are key to illuminating characteristics of effective learning. The following two encounters illustrate how playing with ideas and relationships with people should be valued equally to children's knowledge of physical object conceptual development.

Encounter: Cassie and the clouds

Cassie, aged six-and-a-half, recounts her afternoon playtime at school:

> Cassie: Mummy I threw a stick up into the sky.
> Mum: Did you, didn't it come back down?
> Cassie: Yes and it had fluff on it.
> Mum: . . . what was the fluff?
> Cassie: Cloud.
> Mum: Wow!!

Here, Cassie is *transforming her emerging understanding* of clouds through imaginative ideas.

Whitebread argues:

> Sternberg . . . distinguished between three kinds of cognitive processes: 'knowledge acquisition components' through which we initially acquire

information, skills and strategies; 'performance components' which enable us to implement learnt cognitive procedures and strategies; and 'meta-components' – higher-order processes used to select and coordinate the activities of the other two components in relation to the task in hand and to plan, monitor and evaluate task performance.

(in Broadhead *et al.*, 2010: 163)

Cassie's higher-order processes, of cloud formations, cloud properties and meteorological conditions, will develop when her experiences are richer, older and more diverse; this is also co-dependent on opportunity, challenge, dynamic exchange with peers and adults and having the sense of 'playing around' with ideas valued as essential to knowledge acquisition.

We have noted encounters of playful and effective learning with open-ended resources, both inside and outside, an enduring level of interest in a natural place outside and an emerging playfulness with abstract ideas. Alice, below, demon-strates what Hakkarainen (2006, in Broadhead *et al.*, 2010: 178) 'points out, [that] play is an intrinsically motivated process with outcomes and developmental effects that are not always immediately visible'.

Encounter: Alice actively achieving what she sets out to do

Alice is 17 months old. She has accompanied her parents to a stranger's garden for a friend's barbeque. After staying close to her parents, she eases to the side of the sand on the builder's tray where I join her, patting sand into a yoghurt pot. The action is repeated many times, and Alice knocks them all down. She then looks to the books placed on the rug and brings them over to me. She particularly likes a small book by Shirley Hughes, *Noisy*, and repeats the word 'baby' when I point to the picture and say the word. I clap to mimic the action of the baby. During the next hour or so, Alice continuously picks up the book, finds the page and claps like the baby, while saying 'baby'. She appears to say 'ball' (there is a ball in the picture), and Mike collects a set of croquet balls from the garage; after playing with me and them for a while, she pulls my finger and leads me down towards the garage, saying 'ball'. She clearly wants more balls to play with. I return saying that we have no more, but the 'game' of leading me down the path takes us to the gravel drive, where we make crunching footsteps. I find a plant pot, and we fill it with stones and small sticks and take it to the sand. Her new activity is leading me back to the drive, and occasionally returning to the baby book.

When we come inside, Alice finds someone else, sitting nearer the door, to lead around the house, collecting keys, objects she likes, and returning to the sitting room. I go and find a basket of soft toys, and she gives each of us a toy to keep us all involved.

Alice, through active exploration of adults, has *transformed a new relationship into a trusting one*.

Alice appears to have achieved what she set out to do, once she was comfortable and at ease in her surroundings. Wardle and Vesty explore the importance of well-being in their chapter (Chapter 2) and underline how important it is to the development and sustenance of learning dispositions: the readiness, willingness and ability to be curious and act on that curiosity. Hedges (in Broadhead *et al.*, 2010: 28) suggests, 'Vygotsky ... believed that children's informal daily interactions in families and communities, provide a bank of everyday or spontaneous experiences to draw on later to develop more formal, scientific, conceptual knowledge.' Her motive was to engage with new adults within the close proximity of her parents. The situation was new, but, with an attuned adult used to not rushing playful exploration, and appropriate resources to hand, Alice began to show an interest, mainly with playing with adults, which she is used to; she is a toddler living with parents and currently does not attend any toddler/nursery groups. She appeared to recognise that she could be the centre of attention, particularly if she directed the timing and range of activities. She was pleased at being understood, smiling often and repeating the word 'baby', accompanied by the action of clapping, in which both the picture baby and the real adult participated. This sense of achievement is recognised by Arnold:

> When a human being is encouraged to follow their deep interests, they literally light up and the satisfaction they demonstrate is obvious to others. When children are 'deeply involved' or demonstrate 'chuffedness', they are making or have made some new connections within the affective and/or cognitive domains.
>
> (Arnold and The Pen Green Team, 2010: 157)

Children's dispositions

Wardle and Vesty explore Laevers' involvement and well-being signals in Chapter 2, where they reinforce that characteristics of effective learning are accompanied and associated with a real and deep sense of intensity and satisfaction observable in children taking the lead, sharing ideas, mastering skills, or being absorbed in flow and time. For practitioners, the challenge is providing the balance and blend of activities and opportunities for individual and group activity, child-led and adult-directed activity, when it appears clear that characteristics of effective learning are more easily observed during experiential and exploratory play, suggestive of more child-led enquiry. We perhaps need to remind ourselves of the relationship between teaching and learning – not 'what am I trying to teach them', but 'in what ways am I encouraging children to learn?' Cousins simply states:

Sonnyboy asked innumerable questions of his very patient teacher and had very strong beliefs about the nature of classroom questions. He lost his sunny smile when she asked questions,which to him, were not real questions which everyone had to puzzle over, but were questions to which the teacher and most of her pupils already knew the answer. In his words to his teacher: 'Why do you keep asking us questions when you know all the answers? Like "What colour is it then?" You can see for yourself it's red, so why do you keep asking?'

(1999: 16)

As Edwards *et al.* (1998: 67) argue, '*What children learn does not follow as an automatic result from what is taught. Rather, it is in large part due to the children's own doing as a consequence of their activities and our resources*' (their italics). Gripton examines this further in Chapter 5.

Gray agrees that:

Because play involves conscious control of one's own behaviour, with attention to process and rules, it requires an active, alert mind. Players do not just passively absorb information from the environment, or reflexively respond to stimuli, or behave automatically in accordance with habit; they have to think actively about what they are doing. Yet, because play is not a response to external demands or immediate biological needs, the person at play is relatively free from the strong drives and emotions that are experiences as pressure.

(2013: 152)

Moran will discuss in Chapter 8 that observing, assessing and documenting children's characteristics of effective learning will generally be easier when the child has not been asked to perform particular tasks that may be unconnected to their current interests and enquiries. We know that Vygotsky suggested that children 'play a head above themselves' in self-motivated play. The characteristics of effective learning embedded within the Early Years Foundation Stage Curriculum (Department for Education, 2012) are finding out and exploring, using what they know in their play, being willing to have a go, being involved and concentrating, keeping trying, enjoying and achieving what they set out to do. It is incumbent on us to afford these possibilities for active learning, for children to become 'life-theorisers' (cited by Hedges in Broadhead *et al.*, 2010: 30). How the child performs, 'the way an activity or practice is carried out is highly important for its developmental effect' (van Oers, in Edwards *et al.*, 2010: 198), underpinning 'the idea of "learning dispositions" [as] one of the newest and most powerful theoretical constellations to be found in early childhood education' (Brooker, in Waller *et al.*, 2011: 83). A positive and curious attitude towards finding things out through practice–error–practice–achievement is how we all learn, from the youngest baby to an older person faced with a new cognitive/ technical challenge: we use what we know and adapt to acquire a different understanding. Katz (2001) concludes:

> Children, all children, are born with the disposition to make sense of their experiences. This is also what scientists do – make sense of experiences by experimenting, by utilizing the scientific process. You can see this disposition even in babies. A 4-month-old will drop a spoon and watch as Grandma picks it up – over and over again. She is a scientist, testing her environment to see what happens.
>
> (in Waller et al., 2011: 85)

A child's project can be within its own time frame. An enduring, deep-level interest may be observed in young children through into adolescence, supported by adult interest, not intervention, and encouraged to emerge. This is most noticeable in one's own children, because of the family context, and a *playful* interest sometimes becomes a lifelong recreation or career influence. Effective practitioners will encourage parents to share their children's engaging interests, so that they can be built upon, as illustrated by Hall in the previous chapter. In our settings, these longer-term projects or enquiries can be less noticeable, because of competing interests, pressures of external demands on our own and the children's time, and because of frequent changes in adult personnel; children attending Steiner schools may be said to benefit from less transition between adult teachers. We should be able to observe, however, the constancy of interests *and* the way that children approach both their own chosen tasks and those framed by adult-led direction, and to what extent we can capitalise and enhance a powerful disposition to learn.

Schematic interests are relatively easy to observe, and many early years practitioners, once 'hooked', become 'schema spotters'; for example, the child who builds high, climbs, seems to draw grids and towers and throws objects into the air to watch their height, drop and trajectory. As Hall and McEwan have intimated, children's interests engage them far more deeply than decontextual-ised activities and can be used to enable them to access a more diverse range of ideas, resources and playmates; this is different from *only* using persistent and habitual forms of repetitive play themes and ideas. Our role is to help children make connections within the learning environment and with other children who have similar but distinct interests, and Moran will caution us to be mindful of 'only finding what we look for'.

It can be a wonderful moment when two or three children are directed to an activity or resources that you have planned, having observed their interests, and you watch (and record) what happens next, as the engaging activity and thinking develop and are sustained. It is then that we begin to see children *project* their future plans and creative ideas.

Provocations

- Where or when can children test your environment?
- Can you identify children with a strong disposition to finding things out in their own way? Who are these children, and how do you use their expertise?
- What appear to be the abiding interests of the children you work with?
- How do you plan for children to extend their interests?
- Ryder identifies the path of a project as an observation of a meaningful experience, asking the children where they want to go with it, exploring the idea with colleagues, playing back the ideas and having conversations with children, taking further ideas and beginning practical aspects of the project, involving parents and community, and threading the project together with learning stories. What might the first or next project be?

References

Arnold, C. and The Pen Green Team (2010) *Understanding Schemas and Emotion in Early Childhood*. London: Sage.

Broadhead, P., Howard, J. and Wood, E. (eds) (2010) *Play and Learning in the Early Years*. London: Sage.

Brooker, L. and Edwards, S. (eds) (2010) *Engaging Play*. Maidenhead, UK: Open University Press.

Cobb, E. (1977) *The Ecology of Imagination in Childhood*. Putnam, CT: Spring Publications.

Cousins, J. (1999) *Listening to Four Year Olds. How They Help Us Plan Their Education and Care*. London: NEYN.

Craft, A. (2002) *Creativity and Early Years Education. A Lifewide Foundation*. London: Continuum.

Dahlberg, G. and Moss, P. (2005) *Ethics and Politics in Early Childhood Education*. London: RoutledgeFalmer.

Dewey, J. (1910) *How We Think*. Boston, MA: DC Heath.

Department for Education (2012) *Statutory Framework for the Early Years Foundation Stage (EYFS)*. Cheshire, UK: Department for Education.

Donaldson, M. (1992) *Children's Minds*. London: Fontana Press.

Edwards, C., Gandini, L. and Forman, G. (eds) (1998) *The Hundred Languages of Children*, 2nd edn. Greenwich, CT: Ablex.

Engeström, Y., Miettenen, R. and Punamaki, R.-L. (eds) (1999) *Perspectives on Activity Theory*. Cambridge, UK: Cambridge University Press.

Gray, P. (2013) *Free to Learn*. New York: Basic Books.

Hughes, B. (2012) *Evolutionary Playwork*, 2nd edn. London: Routledge.

Rogoff, B. (1990) *Apprenticeship in Thinking. Cognitive Development in Social Context*. Oxford, UK: Oxford University Press.

Ryder, D. (unpublished) Elemental play: More than sand and water.

Waller, T., Whitmarsh, J. and Clarke, K. (eds) (2011) *Making Sense of Theory and Practice in Early Childhood. The Power of Ideas*. Maidenhead, UK: Open University Press .

5

Playing with thinking

Catherine Gripton

Play is diverse and fluid and rightly beyond the control of adults. Creative and critical thinking is similar in its ownership and variety, but is more internal. As such, creative and critical thinking could be deemed to be playing within. Playing with thinking is about exploring thinking and 'threads of thinking' (Nutbrown, 2006). Exploration needs time, space, stimulation and permission to go in all directions, as indicated in the previous chapter. Thinking is the embodiment of possibilities; through creative thinking, we create possibilities. Through critical thinking, we consider these possibilities, how to pursue, filter, refine and explore them. Creative and critical thinking can interplay reflexively in a fluid relationship.

Assessing children's thinking is fundamentally about reporting upon *how* they learn and *how* they achieve learning, and so does not require quantifying or quality statements; we are describing the nature of the routes, not the journey time or destination. This is contextual and evolving, can be practised, developed and reflected upon by children and practitioners. Attention to children's thinking when observing child-initiated activity reveals much about their learning and supports practitioners in gaining a deep knowledge of the child. This builds a complex and distinct picture, where patterns, preferences – often subconscious – and approaches appear. In reporting upon creative and critical thinking when documenting learning, we are providing information on our interpretation of how each unique child learns, and this is explored further in the final chapter. Attention to thinking in assessment does more than prompt us to include how a child learns; it urges us to consider how our provision provides the landscape for thinking. It challenges us to value and provide for playing with thinking. Our provision extends beyond the concrete, external and physical to the internal, as we strive to provide the thinking playground.

Higher-order thinking skills – for example, creative, evaluative and analytical thinking (Krathwohl, 2002) – are essential for all humans and are part of the thinking that we all do every day. They are not just for special projects, life crises or crossroads; they provide navigation through life, support efficiency, keep us safe, help us work together and provide enjoyment; they open up possibilities. In order to facilitate children's playing with thinking, we can take what we know about play and apply it to thinking. Practitioners understand the need for children to initiate and have ownership of their own play, to have time, space and opportunity to feel secure. Children need to feel that their play is important and valued and, although purposeful, it does not need to have a predetermined outcome or end point. These principles can be similarly applied to thinking, where, as children explore and play with thinking, they create and explore many possibilities. These might be usefully considered as a manifesto for thinking, or the 'rights of a thinker', in a similar way to the 'rights of a reader' (Pennac, 2006).

This manifesto may offer us an opportunity to consider children's rights to abandon a thought or line of thinking, or have preferred ways of thinking or of acting to support thinking, including talking and repeating trains of thought. Children can think in any order and from any starting point, sometimes not knowing the answer, or they can have an opinion and be intuitive and take risks in thinking, including guessing. We need to offer children the opportunity to give several answers to a question or suggest several solutions to a problem, and to use different tools, mechanisms or communication methods to respond to problems or questions, as these may support thinking differently. Children, and their adults, should be able to think in many different ways, have time to think and *be viewed as thinkers*.

Children are naturally competent learners (Fisher, 2013) and need the opportunities and scope to use different types and forms of thinking in their learning and to apply these in a variety of contexts. They need to feel that the thinking process is valued and valuable.

> Younger and more disadvantaged students are held accountable for basic skills, whereas higher order thinking skills are seen as part of upper school curricula, or worse still, optional extras. We argue that this is absurd; thinking and reasoning should be part of the curriculum from the earliest years, and indeed fostering effective reasoning should be the main responsibility of schools.
>
> (Brown and Campione, 1990: 109)

Creative and critical thinking can be overlooked when considering young children's thinking. Notions of stages of development, hierarchies of thinking and readiness thresholds can lead to a perception that such thinking is purely in the realm of older children and adults. Similarly, such thinking can be perceived to be infrequent and specialised, exclusively for specific types of task – whether large scale, abstract, theoretical or within individual curriculum areas – which are often single solution and set by adults. Alternatively, and perhaps most worryingly, such higher-order thinking can be considered to be the behaviour of the 'high-ability' or 'gifted', with associated issues of the reliability and nature of the criteria upon which such judgements are made. Where creative and critical thinking are considered the habits of mind of only the higher-attaining children, there is a very real danger of widening the attainment gap. Expectations, questions and activities that develop, attend to and encourage these types of thinking become the everyday educational experience of only those who are already perceived to be succeeding educationally. With any of the above perceptions, or a multiplicity of these, there is the potential to miss observable evidence of such thinking in the everyday activities of all children and, therefore, to limit possibilities for such thinking through our practice, in terms of provision and interaction. There are, therefore, inherent dangers hiding in some practitioner models, images and perceptions of children and childhood. As individuals and groups of practitioners, we need to explore what we believe about children's thinking and tune our observation skills to see evidence of these types of thinking in the activity of all children, including very young children and those identified as having special educational needs, as Hall has previously intimated. Arguments about the nature of thinking are superseded, for educators, by the impact of our beliefs upon children.

Scaffolding playing with thinking

Developing children's thinking is about creating a thinking ethos or environment, as much as it is about individual thinking skills (Fisher, 1999). Creative thinking is supported by resources and provision within the physical learning environment, which allow and provide opportunities for representation and connections. Such physical provision needs to be open ended and diverse, to enable the child to make regular, varied and complex connections between resources and activities. Such provision, if in sufficient quantities, can contain such a large number of possibilities that they appear to be almost infinite. Block play is an example of such provision.

Encounter: Stephanie and the blocks

Stephanie (5 years old) started building using small, wooden unit blocks, as she often chose to do. She worked quietly, selecting blocks from the shelves to fit. She used base-plate blocks to create floors and, over several sessions, created a building that looked like a skyscraper. Each floor was created out of different shaped blocks, with the third floor from the top made out of bridge-shaped pieces turned end on, so that circular windows were created. Some floors contained pillars in the middle, and others did not. She changed the roof design several times over further sessions, each time collaborating with a different child. Stephanie was the quieter child of the pair on each occasion. One day, the roof was particularly pointy, with many wedge-shaped bricks pointing upwards. From the second day of construction, natural objects and small pieces of fabric had been added to the building. A pine cone sat in each of the six round windows for a time. Sometimes, small-world figures were added for imaginative role-play, but tidied away at the end of each session. On the fourth day, the pine cones, conkers and pebbles were removed, and small-world animals were added to the building. Each floor had one or two types of animal, with pigs now nestled in the round windows. The sheep, on a lower floor, were separated by small unit blocks making pens, with three in the larger ones and two in the smaller ones. Bricks and objects were added and removed by other children across the sessions, including quite a noisy set of toy cars, driven enthusiastically by two 3-year-olds who added a ramp to the first floor. Stephanie smiled at them as they drove their cars around the building and carefully righted bricks knocked down by the pair, after they had driven away. She left the ramp in place, but added animals to it, all facing the same way, in a line that extended across the carpet. At tidy-up time, she and her co-constructors tidied away the bricks on the floor and many of the smaller objects on the building (but not all). After a number of days, Stephanie went to do different activities, occasionally looking over to the block area, where other children continued to adapt and play with the building, often smiling before continuing with her activities.

The encounter with Stephanie provides much insight into how to provide for children's thinking. She was not making one structure, and there was not a sustained grand plan. The joy and challenge were in the adaptation and transformation. To be able to play with thinking, the child needs an environment in which exploration without a known end point is valued. Where children are asked to plan their child-initiated activity or are asked to articulate their goal while playing, children are encouraged to be product oriented. They feel that their activity should have adult validation to be valuable, and their work needs to have some currency in the adult domain. Perhaps in a similar way to abstract artworks, defining 'what it is' or 'what it is meant to be' is less important than how it makes you feel, what it could be or how it connects with you as an individual. Stephanie's comfort with others playing with and adapting her structure and, ultimately, her being comfortable to move on from it, emotionally and physically, are supported by the environment. She is secure in the knowledge that the structure can remain intact and 'left out' at the end of each session, and that she can return to it every session, if she chooses to. This is not always the case with block play, which, for reasons of space, can often be in a multi-purpose carpet and block area, with blocks tidied away after each session. In a setting where children are encouraged or required to access areas on rotation, this would be similarly difficult. This security supports her in sharing the structure with others and allowing others to access it, applying their own creative thinking. She is supported in not seeking instant gratification from her play but in exploring her ideas at a deeper level, creating, filtering, evaluating and following possibilities.

The activity is ultimately rich, owing to the complexity and depth of the thinking that it scaffolds, which, although enabled by the environment, came fundamentally from within Stephanie herself. Ultimately, what the encounter with Stephanie demonstrates is that her creativity was not in conflict with the creativity of the other children; that freedom can enrich the freedom of others, rather than inhibit it.

Having time and space to explore and play with thinking is important, both in the short and long term, for 'possibility thinking', creativity (Craft, 2002; Cremin *et al.*, 2013) and through autonomy, agency and self-determination (Burnard *et al.*, 2006). This is an important feature of the encounter with Stephanie, where time is available for Stephanie to continue the activity until she is ready to leave it, rather than it having to prematurely leave her. Completing an activity by the clock, perceived as an adult constraint, rather than when it feels right can prohibit engagement with larger projects requiring deeper thinking and can be frustrating for children, particularly where play in the home environment is not so constricted (Cousins, 1999). Time is provided for Stephanie, even though it is in regular, shorter sessions, punctuated with other activities, such as lunch-time, group times and going home. Although it could be argued that these other activities are a barrier or an interruption to play, here they appear to be actually supporting creative and critical thinking, as the building is re-evaluated each time she returns to it, supported by creative stimuli from the intervening period. The need for routine, organisation and adult-led activities are not in conflict with her play, as she is able to return to her building and develop it over an extended period of time. Depth of engagement was prioritised over breadth of engagement, which enabled her and her peers to engage in higher-order thinking.

In the very short term, time can also be a factor in whether children engage in deeper levels of thinking. Impulsivity is the enemy of deep thinking (Fisher 2012) and can lead to incorrect, 'first-connection' type answers, particularly for children up to age 5 (Beck *et al.*, 2011). As practitioners, we are aware of the need to give children thinking time before expecting an answer to our questions; perhaps we should also wait for more than one answer. A child's first thought is rarely their best thought and is certainly not their only thought. Perhaps a third, fourth or fifth answer will be more considered, be informed by greater reasoning, critical thinking and 'thinking aloud'. As an adult, this seems to me to be particularly natural in group conversation. In waiting for a space in the conversation, we get thinking time, and the point we are about to make gets refined, changes or develops, including how to express it, how to interject with a more reasoned, salient and succinct point when we make it. This may not be necessarily similar for younger children, as it relates to social experience, working memory and the ability to hold two or more ideas and switch between them, but it suggests that, for older children, group conversations might support thinking time. It also suggests that, in paired discussions, providing thinking time and several answers might support possibilities for connections in thinking; sustained shared conversations are explored further by Brown's in Chapter 7. Providing different ways of responding might also be helpful, as this can delay the response and so provide greater opportunity for higher-order thinking.

Through questioning, practitioners can prompt and promote thinking. They also model curiosity and encourage children's questioning. The type of question is crucial to the type of thinking required by the child and can limit as well as enable possibilities in thinking. Where this questioning frequently limits possibilities, it can also limit the types of question children ask adults, each other and themselves. Our answering of questions can be similarly limiting. Under time and other pressures, where we give immediate, short or simplified judgements or perceived facts, presented as unproblematic answers, we model this as the appropriate amount and depth of thinking required and, therefore, model poor habits of mind. This can negatively enhance the power differential between adult and child, with adults as holders and transmitters of knowledge and not as meaning makers or learners themselves. Children's experiences of questions communicate much to them about the thinking expected of them. This can lead to anticipation of such questions, promoting creative and critical thinking – without the presence of an adult – and an atmosphere that is conducive to thinking.

As practitioners, we support children's thinking through supporting their language development. Thinking is linked to, but not limited by, talk and is often mediated through talk, which can become 'inner speech' (Vygotsky, 1962). As practitioners, we can support children in making this internal–external connection by making thinking visible. Modelling, encouraging and valuing the vocabulary of thinking are important aspects of this. In the encounter with Lily-Mae and Grace, the children have created their own word to converse with each other about thinking and to think together.

Encounter: Lily-Mae and Grace 'jumagine'

Twins Lily-Mae and Grace were 4 years old. Their mother heard them using the word, 'jumagine' regularly while talking or playing and assumed they meant 'imagine' or 'just imagine'. She tried to correct them, particularly Grace, who seemed to have started it off, with Lily-Mae picking it up almost immediately. One day Mum asked her, 'Do you mean "imagine if . . .?"'. Grace replied, 'no' and continued playing with Lily-Mae. Over several months, Mum tried to listen carefully for when the word was used by the children, to ascertain the context in which they were using it and, therefore, their precise meaning. She intended to correct them on this language error, as she was conscious that they were due to start school in September. Despite Mum's best efforts, she was unable to work out exactly what the word meant, despite the twins using it frequently and seeming to understand the other's intentions perfectly. They used it when talking about hypothetical things; for example, 'Jumagine if there was a giant fighting baby in the garden'. They also used it to comment on their interpretation of real-world situations, 'Jumagine the cat in the picture wants to get the wool'. They also used it in a variety of play contexts, including (but not exclusively) imaginative role-play, for both agreeing the context and discussing why things are happening. 'Jumagine you are my servant and a dog', 'jumagine the shark is frightened of the whale' and 'jumagine we are sad because . . .'. There was rarely an 'if' after the 'jumagine' in sentences. Eventually, Mum tried again and suggested to them that they meant 'imagine' or 'pretend', and Lily-Mae firmly denied this, 'No, no, no, it doesn't mean that!'. Mum then asked what 'jumagine' meant. Grace seemed frustrated and annoyed by the question and responded, 'it means jumagine!'. Mum slowly realised that the word was theirs. Over time, she felt that the word was less important than the communication of thinking and, therefore, learning that it facilitated. Two years later, the twins are still regularly using 'jumagine', in conversations with each other and sometimes with others too.

The encounter might suggest that dialogue about thinking sits within a shared arena. It requires space, strong relationships, shared understanding and shared tools, of which language is often an important element. The twins in the encounter resist adult-world interpretations and impositions. They feel ownership of their word, feel its value for their everyday play and conversations and are unwilling to relinquish it. They are using it as a tool to express, to discuss and to engage in shared thinking. Activities that encourage recall of thinking and verbalisation of thinking are supportive of learning, as they bring thinking to the fore.

Essentially, there is a reflexive and fluid symbiotic relationship between thought and action (Bruner, 1986), with intelligence encompassing body and mind through embodied cognition (Claxton, 2012). When assessing children, we are assessing the external representations of their internal thinking, rather than the thinking itself. Through supporting children in verbally representing thinking, we are better able to understand and, therefore, support the internal development of thinking. Modelling the language of thinking is important within modelling thinking and modelling ourselves as thinkers. Our self-concept as thinkers is a crucial element within this that can be communicated to the children through everyday experiences, such as where we place ourselves within the physical learning environment (Gripton, in Woods, 2013). Although talk is important in developing a language of thinking, it is important to remember that this language is diverse and not limited to spoken language (Danko-McGhee and Slutsky, 2007). Through representation, symbolism and action, children communicate their thinking, and, through assessment, we can truly hear and receive this communication.

In assessing children's thinking, we need to remember that these are external representations of internal working. In education, we can reclaim 'behaviour' as a term, so that it no longer relates to discipline but is part of the vocabulary with which we share and reflect upon the observed evidence of children's thinking. We need to do more than just consider whether our environment and practice provide opportunities and support for creative and critical thinking; we must also consider whether they provide opportunities and support for *all* children's creativity and critical thinking. We seek to enable and empower children with their thinking for their learning now and for establishing habits of mind for the future and, each as a unique thinker, to immerse them in a thinking culture (Vygotsky 1978).

Critical thinking

Critical thinking is an important, everyday aspect of thinking that can be perceived as being essentially about questioning, curiosity and enquiry. It is about looking beyond the immediate and superficial. In this way, babies engage in critical thinking when they explore objects by looking at them repeatedly, explore how they feel using their mouths and respond to sounds. They subconsciously act upon a natural instinct to discover and know more, to go beyond the initial experience. Critical thinking varies greatly in terms of complexity and sophistication. This relates to the extent to which the individual explores beyond the immediate; the number, type and depth of the levels beyond the superficial that are considered; and the connections between these. Critical thinking at these deeper levels extends to the questioning of fundamental underlying assumptions. The development of critical thinking is evident in children's actions, conversations and play; an example of this is when children begin repeatedly to ask, 'why, why, why', to probe further where, previously, they might have accepted initial answers more readily.

Although we are all critical thinkers, it is essential that children are educated in critical thinking (Facione, 1990), and that critical thinking is supported across all aspects of education, including the amelioration of inhibiting factors that might reside outside the agency of individual practitioners. Critical thinking has much potential to simultaneously open up and review possibilities in learning. It is purposeful and supports many dispositions of effective learning, such as perseverance, self-regulation and honesty, through open explanation of reasoning and evidence. In considering critical thinking as reflective, there are dangers in perceiving it as a 'stepping back', where this might suggest detachment and emotionless rationality. Emotion both shapes and is shaped by critical thinking. The bond between critical thinking and emotion is often underrepresented (Moon, 2008). It is more important to make this connection when considering, and also assessing, young children's learning. In this way, relationships and feelings of emotional security are essential to create and capture possibilities for critical thinking.

Creative thinking

Perceptions of creativity present a potential barrier to assessment, provision and interaction that support creative thinking. Creative thinking is a less tangible aspect of creativity than physical creations and can lead to an over-emphasis upon arts and creative products in the assessment and development of young children's creativity. As social processes are so important in creativity (Faulkner *et al.*, 2006), this can also lead to difficulty in documenting learning for individual children, where systems are more aligned to individual than group assessment. We are all essentially creative, as we all engage in creative thinking. We are born creative, with emergent creativity evident in the youngest babies (Bruce, 2004; Duffy, 2006), as illustrated by McEwan in Chapter 1.

Practitioner self-concept with regards to creativity is more than a level of confidence; it is about the nature of creativity and our role in nurturing it. The distinction between creative teachers and teaching for creativity (National Advisory Committee on Creative and Cultural Education, 1999) is a useful one when considering how to develop children's creative thinking. Although the two are not discrete or in opposition (Jeffrey and Craft, 2004), the link between a practitioner's view of creativity and their own creativity is significant in the creativity facilitated and attuned to in their practice. Where adults view creativity as being concrete, creative thinking might become quite disconnected from creativity altogether. Indeed, creative activities should develop creative thinking as well as creative skills (Taggart *et al.*, 2005). Creativity should be 'life-wide' (Craft 2002) and be across all aspects of provision and all aspects of learning.

Creative thinking is fundamentally about making connections and finding solutions and is infinitely broad and complex. Bringing creative thinking into reality is how children create their own possibilities for learning, where possibilities become real. We need, therefore, to create a playground for creative thinking where this can occur in ways that we might not foresee. Space, both physical and intellectual, to explore and build creative thinking is limited by adult-led goals, objectives and outcomes-driven provision. Although creativity could be seen as in conflict with an improvement-agenda- or standards-led system, improvement is both the greatest use and significant outcome of creative thinking (De Bono, 1992).

As practitioners, we can support the development of children's everyday creative thinking through providing for possibilities that explore the extremes of their creativity. Children need opportunities to imagine, wonder and generalise, to embrace the impossible and the infinite. Activities, such as in the encounter with Zico, can provide structures to ensure that these activities are visible in the setting and a place to anchor or focus ongoing creative thinking, from home and school environments, and bring it into the physical world.

> ## Encounter: Zico's marvellous invention
>
> In 7-year-old Zico's class, the children had 'My marvellous inventions' exercise books. The class would draw pictures and diagrams, write explanations and label their inventions in these books. Sometimes, the teacher would set a problem or provide a specification, but more often this would be a completely open activity, and the children's inventions would be very diverse, creative and often surprising to their teacher. One week, Zico told his teacher that he had an idea ready in his head. Zico had to wait until the next day for an opportunity to put his invention into his book. He drew a wall with wings, labelled it and wrote the title, 'The flying wall'. Underneath the picture, he explained his thinking in writing. He thought that a movable wall would be useful in school for many different reasons. His many uses included: in the school hall to make two smaller rooms, in the classroom when he was getting distracted by other children, to make the room bigger when using construction and to make a quiet room for reading a book. 'It can be used to make rooms bigger and smaller', he announced triumphantly.

The book for inventions in the encounter appears to create an arena and permission for creativity and, moreover, the expectation of creativity. This supports children in embracing the impossible and facilitates the following of possibilities, without being stifled at the earliest stages by the need for speedy decisions or compliance with externally imposed rules and limitations, often by adults and real-world concerns. Creative thinking is indeed innate (Duffy, 2006), and it is significant in well-being, as suggested by Wardle and Vesty, not only for its cathartic, escapist and aspirational potential, but also in meeting our needs and in its connection to other aspects of thinking. Creativity is how we generate the notions, ideas and, fundamentally, the possibilities to which we apply our critical thinking. It is the constant interplay between the two, internally and externally, that moves us forwards, conceptualises the problem and supports us in solving it.

Problem solving and decision-making

Problem solving can provide purpose and context for thinking. It can bring individual thinking into the shared domain and into the experience of children. As such, it holds much potential for assessment of learning, without problems becoming activities that are adult-led and determined by adult priorities. Problem solving is an approach rather than an activity. In conceptualising problem solving as different to trouble-shooting or mistake correction, we might perceive solutions as a continuum of possibilities, rather than a fixed point. A problem can then be comfortably returned to, with solutions for now being different to solutions forever. As a mindset, problem solving encourages children to see possibilities and know that there is more to know.

Problem solving can be considered as both the product and synthesis of creative and critical thinking, but it goes further than this. Within problem solving, there is a complexity and tension, the wrestling within which lie endless possibilities for learning. There is much potential here for argument, verbal and non-verbal, to reveal, shape, support and challenge thinking and also values and beliefs (Kuhn, 1992).

Encounter: Chloe, Kayley and Violet at snack time

Three children sat around a table waiting for a snack; I shared the crisps one at a time on to three plates, counted again to find that there were seven crisps on each plate, and there were two remaining in the bag. I broke the crisps, putting two small pieces on one plate and a larger piece on each of the other two plates. As I put the plates on the table in front of the children, their eyes skittered quickly around each other's and then their own plates. Violet was the first to cry, 'it's not fair, she's got more than me', followed quickly by a howl from Chloe, saying something similar. Kayley, the third child, smirked to herself while putting crisps into her mouth as quickly and quietly as possible. I realised that there were three options available to me on the next occasion: I could not give any crisps, as an opportunity to learn about expected behaviour, share out the whole crisps and then throw away (or eat) the remaining ones, or I could repeat what I did last time and break the remaining crisps into sixths. I decided against any of these options and put the packet of crisps in the middle of the table. The children looked at me, then at the bag. Chloe shrugged her shoulders and opened the bag, offering one to Violet and then one to Kayley, before taking one herself and popping it in her mouth and returning the bag to the middle. This continued in a similar way each time: they all waited for the others to finish eating before sharing again; the order sometimes varied, and they agreed for one round to take two each, but each child ate the same number of crisps. When they got to the final two, Chloe declared that there were only two left, and they all looked at each other. Violet, who had spotted an available toy train across the room, said 'I don't mind' and ran off to play with the train, leaving Chloe and Kayley to eat the final two crisps. Over the next few times they shared food, their solutions became more sophisticated, with estimations of the total quantity and counting, rather than turn taking, to keep check of how many each had eaten. They often chose to have different quantities, but all seemed happy that this was their decision, and they sometimes negotiated foods between them to get more of a preferred food and less of another.

In the encounter, the original issue was not so much about the number of crisps they each had received, or their lack of understanding of equivalent fractions, but that they perceived unfairness in the actions of an adult with whom they had a significant relationship. In trying to solve the problem for them, I had created unhappiness rather than avoided it and had missed an opportunity for children to engage in higher-order thinking. In relinquishing ownership of the solution and replacing this with trust, the children and their thinking were valued. This created the time and space to explore ideas, think of and share their own solutions *to think creatively* and evaluate their solutions.

As exemplified in the encounter with Chloe, Kayley and Violet, adults with the best intentions can be too helpful to children when problem-solving opportunities arise. Parents and practitioners can solve problems for children, particularly where argument may be involved. Adults also might ask children to solve problems where the solution is predetermined, and the child is guessing at the 'correct' answer, often with the knowledge that this is not a genuine problem. It is also possible that practitioners can accidentally solve problems that other practitioners are leaving for children to solve. With this scenario, a whole-team approach is important, with a shared awareness that the rich learning opportunities for children in problems are important. Planning fosters and utilises flexibility of thought (McCormack and Atance, 2011), and, therefore, children need to make their own plans and decisions, as these are important in supporting children's development as thinkers.

Children making decisions about their own education and being more involved with and inside the process of education is an important and noble goal. It values and promotes children's thinking. If we are to genuinely listen to children's voices, and we should, for all the reasons outlined by Moran (in Woods, 2013), then children need to experience and be adept at creative and critical thinking. This will support development of thinking, as the arena and imperative are provided for possibilities within which ideas can be created and evaluated. There are, however, inherent dangers here. Where children are making decisions, these decisions need to be genuine and authentic. One could argue that the appearance of power and voice where it does not exist is more damaging than no voice or power at all, as it teaches the child to express their ideas without expectation that they will be enacted: their voice is heard but ignored. Children are astute at spotting this, as the encounter with Charlotte suggests.

Encounter: Charlotte and the game cards

Charlotte was on the school council for her primary school, but became disillusioned with it. She explained:

> The school council has no real power, we make decisions and suggestions but they are only taken up if they are what the teachers wanted to do anyway. We made a decision to have a club for sharing game cards at lunchtime but it was ignored because the grownups think it is not worth the effort. It IS worth it to us and we would've made it work. The teachers just didn't want it!

Where adults filter children's problem solving and decision-making, the message to children is clear. Where only certain outcomes of decision-making are possible, then, from the outset, this needs building into the problem that they seek to solve. Charlotte appears to be frustrated by the dismissal of a solution that she believes to be a valid one. The adults in this encounter probably had sensible concerns about potential negative outcomes for some children arising from the idea. Perhaps they were not really seeing the positive benefits as the children did, and as such the idea appeared to be less viable when even minor obstacles presented. Perhaps the adults' greater life experience enabled them to see future problems more clearly, although this could also be making assumptions (perhaps based upon similar experiences with different children).

Thinking essentially creates possibilities. As practitioners, we need to support children in engaging in possibility creation. The power of thought sets us free, but also creates possibilities of failure and mistakes (Dewey, 1910); thinking is, therefore, emancipating but also risky. Supporting and nurturing children to be able to engage in mental and emotional risk taking is, therefore, an essential aspect of the practice of working with young children. Practitioners have been enabling, supporting, encouraging and providing for children's creative and critical thinking for many years. It is essential and, therefore, important that there is continual reflection upon practice and provision in terms of how we enable and encourage these types of thinking, in particular through problem solving, reasoning and argument. This reflection supports us in affirming our rationale for provision that develops children's thinking.

Play, as an active representation of the inner life of the child (Froebel, 1885), is essential in the development of thinking (Taggart *et al.*, 2005). In upholding children's right to play, we are respecting them and supporting their development as thinkers and, therefore, effective learners. Activities such as sorting or story times, which include thought-provoking questions, are important for developing children's thinking, but could be eroded by a focus upon reading and counting, leading to number naming and decoding taking precedence. The perception that higher-order thinking is based *within* rather than *upon* 'basic skills' is supportive of early years practice. It supports us in creating and seeking the opportunities to assess *how* the children are learning, as well as *what* they are learning. This is essentially an issue of perception, as our views are shaped by pathological and psychological perceptions of child development (Dahlberg *et al.*, 2006). It is important to perceive development in creative and critical thinking, not as a linear or staged progression, with higher or lower attainment, but more as snowflakes, where the size is less important than form and how this form is changing and unique. Creative and critical thinking is a key way in which children extend and develop their play and learning through the creation and interpretation of possibilities. Through the creation of a thinking culture, we can continue to challenge and support real, deep and authentic learning that will serve children and society well, now and in the future.

Provocations

- Reflecting upon different models of learning, what potential for supporting critical thinking, problem solving and creativity do different models of learning encompass? In what ways does thinking, creative and critical thinking in particular, form part of your image of the child and of childhood?

- How long do you wait before expecting a response to a question? Could you practise increasing this time?

- When do children have the opportunity to give more than one answer or solution? Does this happen in a range of contexts?

- Where do you see yourself problem solving *for* children? Could you hand the problem over to the children, and how might you do this?

- How could a thinking culture be created in a setting? How would you recognise a setting with a thinking culture?

- What types of thinking do the questions you ask prompt? Which questions do you ask that promote children's higher-order thinking?

- How can you support children in making their thinking visible, including developing a vocabulary to articulate their thinking?

- Where do you or could you provide discrete sessions or opportunities that focus upon developing children as thinkers? Where might opportunities to extend thinking develop within all activities?

- In your setting, what opportunities do children have to solve problems and make decisions about the setting? Do all children have a voice in this, and are children's solutions and decisions valued?

- How can you support children in asking questions that promote higher-order thinking?

- How do you perceive yourself as a thinker? How does this impact upon your work with children?

References

Beck, S.R., Carroll, D.J., Brunsdon, V.E.A. and Gryg, C.K. (2011) 'Supporting children's counterfactual thinking with alternative modes of responding', *Journal of Experimental Child Psychology*, 108: 190–202.

Brown, A.L. and Campione, J.C. (1990) 'Communities of learning and thinking, or a context by any other name', in Kuhn, D. (ed.) *Developmental Perspectives on Teaching and Learning Thinking Skills*, New York: Karger.

Bruce, T. (2004) *Cultivating Creativity: For Babies, Toddlers and Young Children*, Abingdon, UK: Hodder Education.

Bruner, J.S. (1986) *Actual Minds, Possible Worlds*, London: Harvard University Press.

Burnard, P., Craft, A., Cremin, T., Duffy, B., Hanson, R., Keene L., Haynes, L. and Burns, D. (2006) 'Documenting "possibility thinking": a journey of collaborative enquiry', *International Journal of Early Years Education*, 14(3): 243–26.

Claxton, G. (2012) 'Turning thinking on its head: how bodies make up their minds', *Thinking Skills and Creativity*, 7: 78–84.

Cousins, J. (1999) *Listening to Four Year Olds: How They Can Help Us Plan Their Education and Care*, London: National Early Years Network.

Craft, A. (2002) *Creativity and Early Years Education: A Lifewide Foundation*, London: Continuum.

Cremin, T., Chappell, K. and Craft, A. (2013) 'Reciprocity between narrative, questioning and imagination in the early and primary years: examining the role of narrative in possibility thinking', *Thinking Skills and Creativity*, 9: 135–51.

Dahlberg, G., Moss, P. and Pence, A.R. (2006) *Beyond Quality in Early Childhood Education and Care: Languages of Evaluation*, London: Routledge.

Danko-McGhee, K. and Slutsky, R. (2007) 'Floating experiences: empowering early childhood educators to encourage critical thinking in young children through the visual arts', *Art Education*, 60: 13–16.

De Bono, E. (1992) *Serious Creativity: Using the Power of Lateral Thinking to Create New Ideas*, London: HarperCollins.

Dewey, J. (2010) *How We Think*, New York: DC Heath.

Duffy, B. (2006) *Supporting Creativity and Imagination in the Early Years*, Buckingham, UK: Open University Press.

Facione, P.A. (1990) *Critical Thinking: A Statement of Expert Consensus for Purposes of Educational Assessment and Instruction. Research Findings and Recommendations*, Newark, NJ: American Philosophical Association.

Faulkner, D., Coates, E., Craft, A. and Duffy, B. (2006) 'Creativity and cultural innovation in early childhood education', *International Journal of Early Years Education*, 14: 191–9.

Fisher, J. (2013) *Starting From the Child: Teaching and Learning in the Foundation Stage*, Berkshire, UK: Open University Press.

Fisher, R. (1999) 'Thinking skills to thinking schools: ways to develop children's thinking and learning', *Early Child Development and Care*, 153: 51–63.

Fisher, R. (2012) *Creating a Community of Enquiry* (INSET for staff), Blessed Robert Widmerpool Primary School, Nottingham, UK, 9 May.

Froebel, F. (1885) *The Education of Man*, New York: A. Lovell.

Jeffrey, B. and Craft, A. (2004) 'Teaching creatively and teaching for creativity: distinctions and relationships', *Educational Studies*, 30: 77–87.

Krathwohl, D.R. (2002) 'A revision of Bloom's Taxonomy: an overview', *Theory into Practice*, 41: 212–18.

Kuhn, D. (1992) 'Thinking as argument', *Harvard Educational Review*. 62(2): 155–78.

McCormack, T. and Atance, C.M. (2011) 'Planning in young children: a review and synthesis', *Developmental Review*, 31: 1–31.

Moon, J. (2008) *Critical Thinking: An Exploration of Theory and Practice*, London: Routledge.

National Advisory Committee on Creative and Cultural Education (1999) *All Our Futures: Creativity, Culture and Education: Report*, London: Department for Education and Employment.

Nutbrown, C. (2006) *Threads of Thinking: Young Children Learning and the Role of Early Education*, London: Sage.

Pennac, D. (2006) *The Rights of the Reader*, London: Walker Books.

Taggart, G., Ridley, K., Rudd, P. and Benefield, P. (2005) *Thinking Skills in the Early Years: A Literature Review*, Slough, UK: NFER.

Vygotsky, L.S. (1962) *Thought and Language*, London: MIT Press.

Vygotsky, L.S. (1978) *Mind in Society: The Development of Higher Psychological Processes*, London: Harvard University Press.

Woods, A. (ed.) (2013) *Child-Initiated Play and Learning: Planning for Possibilities in the Early Years*, London: Routledge.

6

Guiding children's participation

Annie Woods

Encounter: Annie with preschool

Over the last 18 months, I have spent many Fridays working alongside two experienced practitioners and different groups of 3- and 4-year-olds outside, in a young woodland, for 3 hours each morning.

After the session this week, one of the last ones I will get to, I mulled over the morning and, as always, felt as calm and happy as I perceived the children had been. It was a typical morning, but remarkable in so many ways, reflections include:

- Sitting on a log while pairs of children counted together, choosing numbers from 16 to 39, to wait before shaking a tambourine to recall children back to the tree; one adult with the other children, two of us on a log, keeping the 'counters' company and exchanging good thoughts about the amazing and purposeful counting.
- A child coming up to ask: 'Annie, what is a 'sted'? One of the adults had suggested he do something *instead*, but it took me a while to work this out. Trying to explain 'instead' to a 4-year-old is quite a challenge, but he really wanted to know.
- A child explaining that a brown butterfly is probably a moth.
- Asking Penny why she liked snails so much. She said it was the circles, her favourite being the brown, white and black stripes. Ah, I replied, the stripe pattern was a spiral. 'Yes, I like the spirals.'
- Sam, who was a little apprehensive of the woodland boundary walk in the overhead-high woodland plants, but was encouraged by joining in on 'we're going on a bear hunt', then along with Charlie suggested they might find a lion, a bear, a penguin, a dinosaur, a monkey . . . the list was long, both in species and time, and it was not until the end of the walk that very specific named dinosaurs emerged. This was evidence of continued thinking, recall and full adult participation in an imaginary world of a range of animals hiding in the woods – not to scare them, but almost as 'friends' walking alongside in unseen jungle.

The focus of this chapter is to consider the elements of participation noted in this encounter and then to really look at how guided participation is the enhanced role that good and effective practitioners can play when they work alongside children and support their characteristics of effective learning. What is the reflective adult recounting here? Physical and emotional *attachment* and *observing* children as they play a game of '1, 2, 3 . . . come back to the tree', a forest school game used to familiarise children with woodland boundaries, as well as a safe measure to ensure children return to a base when necessary; a semantic discussion with a 4-year-old, as tools of language are *explained* and used, then, later, enhancement of description to engage a child's interest in snails. This was a sustained interest, and every week snails were found, researched and cared for. There was also an attuned adult *recognising* some anxiety felt by a child in grasses and plants that looked impenetrable, but *knowing* a song that the children enjoyed to help allay any fears and then supporting the children's wild-animal imaginings in a very gentle woodland, having fun conjuring up every animal they could remember – arctic, jungle, desert and extinct! Reading this, you will recognise the everyday – the physical, emotional, linguistic and cognitive participative role of practitioners.

Quality interactions

It may be suggested that, at times, we do not celebrate or reflect upon the everyday that seems to make the difference between an adequate and an outstanding provision. Katz (1995: 65) states:

> Dispositions are best learned when they are modelled for children by those around them – by teachers who think about their uncertainties and their problem-solving. If teachers want their young pupils to have robust dispositions to investigate, hypothesise, experiment, and so forth, they might consider making their own such intellectual dispositions more visible to the children.
>
> (cited by Brooker in Waller *et al.*, 2011: 88)

In the updated Ofsted *School Inspection Handbook* (2013), the *quality* of teaching is embraced, with key phrases positively reminding us that:

> Inspectors must not expect teaching staff to teach in any specific way. Schools and teachers should decide for themselves how to teach so that children are engaged in lessons, acquire knowledge and learn well [p. 121]; when observing and judging teaching, inspectors must be guided by the *response and engagement* [my italics] of [children] and evidence of how well they are learning [p. 123]; and whether teaching engages and includes all [children], with work that is challenging enough and that meets their individual needs

[p. 124]. [Children's] responses demonstrate sufficient gains in their knowledge, skills and understanding, and teachers monitor and use the information well to adapt their teaching us[ing] questioning and discussion [p. 125].

The dispositions highlighted by Katz and discussed within this book should sustain us in any question and reflection of the quality of our interactions with children. Hedges cites Rogoff, who explains that:

> Guided participation involves adults or children challenging, constraining and supporting children in the process of posing and solving problems – through material arrangements of children's activities and responsibilities as well as though interpersonal communication, with children observing and participating at a comfortable but slightly challenging level.
>
> (Hedges, 1990: 18, in Brooker and Edwards, 2010: 41)

The first encounter involved me in accepting that, because it was brown, the butterfly was probably a moth. Later, in the home garden, I saw 'a moth', consulted a guide and found that it was a butterfly, the same species as in the woodland. The child had been comfortable in her knowledge and acknowledged by the adult. I stored the new knowledge with the guide *ready* to use in the next visit to the woods. The approach was not to tell the child she had been wrong, but to express my own uncertainty that what she saw may have been a butterfly, using the guide and opportunity for a butterfly hunt . . . *if* the child was interested to do this. Alternatively, when engaging in conversation on the logs, an opportunity to use the woodland guide would arise, and the mistake would be uncovered. Many of the children use the logs for rest and conversation and, although they rarely take the chance to look at non-fiction books within the preschool environment, are often keen to use the photographs, index and comparative picture data to catalogue what they have seen, using the books, in the *real* outdoor context.

Sometimes, it is so dark under the canopy of wet trees that we use hand-held and head torches to look at books – 'not teaching in any specific way' (Ofsted, 2013). It is interesting here that Brooker (in Waller *et al.*, 2011) further argues that:

> The acquisition of knowledge and skills, Katz . . . points out, does not mean that they will be used and applied (listening skills do not make children listen; reading skills do not make children read). Instructional processes designed to *teach* skills may undermine the disposition to use those skills (drill in reading may not produce readers, but may instead discourage reading).
>
> (p. 88)

I have also been open about expressing my uncertainty, challenging the children to accept their own. The woodland, here, was the material environment;

we can also reflect these experiences within our provision and use photographs of the moth/butterfly and guidebooks to support children's connections, not *presenting* thirty cut-out butterfly shapes for 'blob prints/symmetry', but perhaps A3 prints of the photographs, appropriate pastels, crayons, paints and pencils and collage materials for freely chosen activity based on what the children had seen themselves and recorded.

Malaguzzi reminds us that:

> [Children] are autonomously capable of making meaning from their daily life experiences through mental acts involving planning, coordination of ideas, and abstraction. Remember, meanings are never static, univocal or final; they are always generative of other meanings. The central act of adults, therefore, is to activate, especially indirectly, the meaning making competencies of children as a basis of all learning.
>
> (in Edwards *et al.*, 1998: 81)

'Getting to know' cultural tools: becoming an apprentice

Rosen's book, *We're Going on a Bear Hunt* (1989), is a favourite of children and practitioners, acted and chanted regularly. It is a familiar cultural artefact in preschools and, thus, has been assimilated into practice. The chant is full of rhythmic refrain, and illustrations depict a family of children led by Dad, overcoming obstacles, facing a fear (bear) and returning home safe and sound. Jordan (in Brooker and Edwards, 2010: 96) tells us that, 'Adults, as the more experienced tool-users and meaning-makers, contribute to learning through their relationships with children, through provision of play opportunities and through interactions that interpret our cultural heritage in support of children's particular funds of knowledge.' The first encounter demonstrated my experience as a 'tool-user', able to use the story to help Sam overcome his fear of the obstacle of very tall plants. He quickly joined in the refrain with two other children, and *their* 'particular funds of knowledge' recreated the story on a number of hilarious levels. We had other obstacles to leap over, crunch through or brush aside, with sleeves held over hands or arms reaching up to avoid the nettles; we also *saw* a number of other animals that, if combined in a new version of *We're Going on a Bear Hunt*, would offer much discussion and laughter. The children joining in were involved in 'authentic play-based learning [. . .] situated in socially and culturally constructed settings and [. . .] mediated by "responsive and reciprocal relationships with people, places and things"' (Hedges, in Brooker and Edwards, 2010: 26). Here, Hedges draws on the *Te Whāriki* (New Zealand Ministry of Education, 1996) curriculum to underline the importance of participative relationships as the basis of guiding inexperienced learners in their developing confidence and skills. The children knew the story, and it was used in a new context – an example of assimilation and co-construction, as Brooker states:

> Cognitive development, in other words, occurs in the course of 'children's everyday involvement of social life' (Rogoff, 1990: 18), including their intent participation in all the activities which they see other children, and adults, performing. Such participation, Rogoff argues, depends for its effectiveness on the *intersubjectivity* [her italics] or 'shared understanding' which exists between the expert and the novice (1990: 71).
>
> (Brooker and Edwards, 2010: p41)

The first encounter, as we have seen, is rich for reflection; Penny, the child interested in snails, has been introduced (or reminded) of the concept of spiral. Edwards *et al.* offer the suggestion that:

> Put more simply, we seek a situation in which the child is about to see what the adult already sees. The gap is small between what each one sees, the task of closing it appears feasible, and the child's skills and disposition create an expectation and readiness to make the jump. In such a situation, the adult can and must loan to the children his judgement and knowledge. But it is a loan with a condition, namely, that the child will repay.
>
> (Edwards *et al.*, 1998: 84)

Penny sustained her interest in snails, repaying the adults with evidence of deep engagement.

Encounter: Penny and the snails

For the past 3 weeks, Penny has set about finding, holding and examining snails. She also picks up slugs and now knows that slugs do not live in shells but excrete slime to enable them to move. She finds very tiny snails and those with distinct patterns on their shells; she begins to notice the spiral pattern. When she picks them up, the snails go back into their shells, and she wants them to crawl . . . I make a suggestion that if she holds her hands still, the snail will usually emerge through warmth and stillness. Penny is too busy on the hunt for more snails and often deposits the found snails in my hand to 'warm them up'. Once emerged, she usually places them on a tree for safety and then is surprised at how far they can climb. Last week, Michael, caught up in her interest, spent a long time creating a nested bed for the snails, and they both placed all the found snails on a log disc before covering them in dry leaves.

Penny has become an expert snail hunter, looking at leaves, on the ground and under logs, and is beginning to consider their survival needs with guided participation. She remains adamant about wanting to pass around a snail at recall time, when children are encouraged to remember their favourite activity of the morning. Through conversation, we are trying to help her understand that the snails are very delicate, and that some children do not like the slime they excrete. She is increasingly fascinated by talking about the spiral pattern, and we may be able to find a way to exploit this interest of hers by involving other children who see patterns in the natural environment. We need to be ready, willing and able ourselves to respond to, and be proactive about, suggestions for enhanced activities; 'The planning is the anticipation of, having the resources ready to follow the child's [own] interests and willingness to interpret and assess this shared learning as it happens' (Woods, 2013: 3).

Importantly, adult readiness reflects Haakarainen's idea (in Engeström *et al.*, 1999: 247) that:

> What seems to be totally independent play of children at the moment was initiated, guided and instructed by perhaps years ago. The adults' own play experiences influence which play themes are selected and how they are set up and guided.

It is interesting to observe interactions between adults and children and where important interactions take place, with Needham (in Waller *et al.*, 2011) adding, 'Studies of children's learning from early infancy onwards draw attention to the nature of the interactions between adults and children as a key indicator of effective learning' (p. 56). An adult familiar with slugs and snails and natural history *is likely to be an effective playmate for a child* interested in snails; an adult who likes constructing train tracks, towers, brick villages and buildings for animals *is likely to be a responsive floor-based practitioner*; an adult apprenticed in the past to a grandparent and the delights of an accessible kitchen *is likely to afford similar possibilities to children*. What we will then observe is:

> transformation of participation in cultural activities. Such a transformation sees a child's performance in culturally valued activities [cooking, gardening, singing rhymes and retelling stories, reading, playing an instrument, for example] change over time from that of novice to that of expert, as a result of drawing on the affordances of the environment, under the guidance of more experienced individuals.
>
> (Brooker, in Brooker and Edwards, 2010: 41)

Here, effective practitioners, working with learners, demonstrate knowledge-in-action and, when applying theoretical concepts to this action, we see evidence of socio- and co-construction, guided participation, apprenticeship, transformation of participation and participatory appropriation, all of which fit with the notion of a community of learners 'in which both adults and children contribute support and direction in shared endeavours' (Rogoff *et al.*, 1996: 389). It can be as simple as the following encounter, or as involved as the subsequent observation of Alice.

Encounter: Lara in the woods

Lara (adult) places a tarpaulin in the clearing and lies down. Andrew lies next to her sucking his thumb. Penny joins them.

> Lara: It's absolutely beautiful. I love the sun dappling through the trees. I like the colours.

The two children look up, silently watching the gentle movement of the leaves above.

Encounter: Alice and the letters

Alice, at 2 years 7 months, had returned from the beach at the end of the day and was restless in the caravan; many adults were talking to each other. I retrieved the 'Red Busy Box', which she had used with two visiting friends earlier in the week. The box contains crayons, chalks, pens, pencils, a range of papers, a colouring book, magic painting books and dot/small square peelable stickers.

Alice took the box of pencils and was interested in making isolated marks on the paper, carefully placing the pencils back into the ridged plastic tray within the box. She noticed the pencil sharpener, and I showed how to use it by turning the pencil and holding the sharpener still. All pencils were sharpened, and with care, and she spent 15 minutes on this task. When she had replaced all the pencils, I showed her the pens with lids – she appeared to enjoy the order and fit of the tools; again, she made isolated marks on paper and she said she would give it to Charles (an adult). I asked if it was a letter, and did she need an envelope? She agreed, and we found one in the box. She carefully inserted the letter, folded to fit, and I showed her how to lick the gum. She then wrote on the envelope, and I asked if the letter needed a stamp? The square stickers were identified and used.

All adults in the caravan were given a letter. Each letter was written on in a different colour pen and each had an envelope, an address and a stamp.

My role was to provide appropriate resources, guide, suggest, support and work within her time frame. The activities lasted over an hour and were calm and child-centred, with encouragement and verbal reward given by all peripheral adults. I had helped her appropriate the cultural practice of letter writing and posting conventions.

Her grandma promised to find more recycled/new envelopes to replenish the box; I also suggested she pick up leaflets and forms for filling in, as these also may be of interest to Alice. My role here was to be ready to extend a possible interest and to help other adults participate in (an informal) community of effective early childhood practice.

This encounter is an example of:

> apprenticeship ... involving active individuals [Alice, me, grandma, peripheral adults] participating with others in culturally organised activity that has as part of its purpose the development of mature participation in the activity by the less experienced people [Alice and her grandma]. The concept of *participatory appropriation* refers to how individuals change through their involvement in one or another activity, in the process of becoming prepared for subsequent involvement in related activities.
>
> (Rogoff, in Hall *et al.*, 2008: 60)

Rogoff further states:

> I see children's active participation itself as being the process by which they gain facility in an activity. As Wertsch and Stone ... put it, 'the process *is* the product'. The participatory appropriation view of how development and learning occur involves a perspective in which children and their social partners are interdependent, their roles are active and dynamically changing, and the specific processes by which they communicate and share in decision making are the substance of cognitive development.
>
> (ibid.: 65–6)

A role-play post office may offer similar opportunities, provided there is adult participatory play, a purpose for sending letters and it is as a result of a provocation – a visit to the local postbox and office, a planned party or event, or perhaps a story that children had enjoyed and ask to be repeated – and where the adult(s) avoid or minimise 'instructional processes by which some knowledge and skills are acquired [which] may themselves damage or undermine the disposition to use them' (Katz, 1993). More effectively, 'caregivers arrange the occurrence of children's activities and facilitate learning by regulating the difficulty of the tasks and by modelling mature performance during joint participation in activities' (Rogoff, 1990: 17).

Children's 'new' ideas

Becoming a postal worker, delivering many letters, affording the possibility of making just one mark on a piece of paper, believing Sam and his friends when they see penguins and dinosaurs and lions in a wood involve us in suspending our own belief and knowledge experiences in order to participate in the world of the learner, experiencing ideas and activities *for the first time*. We know these animals cannot cohabit or even exist in the same place at the same time, but we must take utmost care in guiding our youngest children, as Gripton has argued in the previous chapter. There is a dichotomy here. Rogoff *et al.* suggest that:

> Children are active constructors of knowledge, and adult involvement is seen as a potential impediment to learning. Children discover reality on their own or through interaction with peers is the ideal: children become the active agents in learning and the adult world is either seen as a passive source of materials or as a negative influence that can stunt the budding of children's own potential. Children are expected to discover and extend the know-ledge, skills and technologies of human history among themselves: adults set up learning environments for the children but should otherwise avoid influencing children's 'natural' course of learning. The challenge is to get the natural learning to correspond with the skills and standards that the community values for the children.
>
> (1996: 395)

Blended learning experiences

The challenge is achieving the balance 'implemented through planned, purposeful play and through a mix of adult-led and child-initiated activity. Children learn by leading their own play, and by taking part in play which is *guided by adults* [my italics]' (Department for Education, 2012). Rogoff *et al.* (1996) see this as a 'pendulum swing', where the more adult-led the activity, the more one-sided the experience may be, with the child a passive rather than active participant. If children feel they are not given choices through guided participation, then their readiness, willingness and ability to participate and then develop their own interests into deeper-level enquiries and gradually take responsibility for their own learning and the group's functioning may remain underdeveloped or perceived as less valued than adult-led activity.

Like Sam earlier, Otis also seemed reluctant to participate, and it is important to acknowledge the role of guided emotional participation in supporting a child to join in and 'confront [. . .] events and experiences' (Edwards *et al.*, 1998: 30).

Encounter: Otis and the deep puddle

Otis has taken some time to settle after his mum has left him to play in the woods with us. He seems reluctant to put on waterproofs, but watches the other children intently as they walk up and down the puddle. He begins to tentatively put his boot into the edge of the squelch. He asks for the waterproof dungarees. He looks at me.

> Otis: Do you know where my feet go? Come and play. Look out! Come in here, you can . . . Can you get me out of here? How much giant steps do I need to do . . .? 1, 2 I need to do 1, 2 . . . 2, 2, 2, 2, 2

Otis is walking up and down the length of the 10-foot muddy puddle, trailing through the watery mud. He goes down on his haunches. He kicks and splashes. I am very close by.

> Otis (to me): watch out for the deeper bits.
> Oh, plow, you come in, go in here. Oh squished, let me go in it, let me have in. I just went straight, turn it.

He is much quicker now, almost running. Two other children join Otis, who is stamping up and down.

> Otis (to me): Let's go and play in that giant piece of water.

Otis has been engaged for over an hour; my participation was engaging rather than guiding, but he may have perceived my presence as an emotional guide for his tentative then growing confidence in the puddle play, as he constantly invited me to participate.

We can agree, here, that, 'The actual interactions between children and their caregivers and peers are nested within the constraints of the available activities and companions' (Rogoff, 1990:87). Jumping puddles, it may be argued, is not a skilled activity, nor may it have cultural value, but it is about curiosity, exploration and courage and is a 'play constant': all children enjoy puddles, arguably through past, present and future generations. If the accompanying adult is ready to get wet and muddy, able to look beyond the washing machine/change of clothes and willing to work at the pace of the child, not only will they make more sense of what it is the children are fascinated by, but they will also increase the value of the activity for the child; they will sense the adult's own interest in their playful learning. Rogoff (in Hall *et al.*, 2008: 70) argues that, 'The investigation of people's actual involvement in activities becomes the basis of our understanding of development rather than simply the surface details that we try to get past.' This encounter also suggests that what practitioners may understand by 'scaffolding' is imperfect. Needham implies that:

> The concept of scaffolding [. . .] developed by Wood and Bruner . . . suggests that children developed more consistent abilities to resolve problems where the adult allowed the child to retain as much control of the process as possible and drew the child's attention to significant aspects of the process. Jordan ... studying preschool teachers involved in interactions, describes an additional distinction in adult–child interactions extending the analysis of scaffolding. She points to improved understanding through co-construction.
>
> (in Waller *et al.*, 2011: 56)

The scaffolding, therefore, seems most effective when it is on the child's terms – instead, spirals, scary and tall plants, moths and butterflies, deepness of puddles –'matched to the level of the child and faded out as the child assumes greater control of what is to be learned *or experienced*' [my italics] (Needham, ibid.). It is worth sitting back to observe interactions between adults and children and consider whether any scaffolding or scaffold activities prioritise a curriculum-based outcome or the child's own goals. Rogoff *et al.* suggest that:

> In adult-run [instruction], the students' role is to enter the adult-defined inquiry rather than to share inquiry with others. Students learn how to solve problems but not how to set them. They can produce correct answers but do not have experience examining how to determine what is correct. They learn how to participate in tasks that are not of their own personal interests and how to be motivated by the teacher but not how to build on or develop their own interests to extend to new and difficult enquiries. Students learn how to be led through tasks but not how to manage themselves or others in inquiry.
>
> (1996: 393)

Stewart (2011: 43) gives us a good example of a teacher planning a role-play area with a piratical theme, 'with the intention that children will develop their verbal narrative ability by acting out a story they have read together', but also acknowledges that 'children bring their own purposes [. . .] at the edge of their capabilities' (ibid.).

Guided participation

We have a dilemma here, faced by many teachers and practitioners, deeply woven within the pedagogical approaches and philosophical purposes of education and, perhaps, the difference between education and schooling. One can agree with Rogoff that:

> Children enter the world embedded in an interpersonal system involving their caregivers and others who are already involved with societal institutions and technologies. Through guided participation with others, children come to understand and participate in the skilled activities of their culture.
>
> (1990: 191)

We can also recognise, however, that, increasingly, our preschool, primary and secondary education provision is a model of transmission of knowledge *to* learners; this chapter urges readers to afford opportunities and possibilities to achieve more than children being 'able to demonstrate that [knowledge] has been encoded and retained' (Rogoff *et al.*, 1996: 390). We may acknowledge here the powerful influence of the Reggio Emilia approach to counter what appears to be the dominance of a one-sided role of schooling. Early years practitioners will recognise 'the hundred languages of children', 'the strength and competence of resilient children' and the reciprocity of adult–child and child–child exchange:

> The mutual involvement of people working on similar issues is part of the social context of creativity. Dialogue, collaboration, and building from previous approaches often provide the catalyst of putting two ideas together that would not have occurred without the need for the individual thinker to carry out, explain, or improve on an approach.
>
> (Rogoff, 1990: 199)

Encounters: collecting rain

1 The woodland was soggy. It seemed to have rained for weeks. The heavy canopy of leaves created a dark and gloomy play space, and we quickly erected roof tarpaulins between trees. The children wore fluorescent jackets and head torches and were excited to run in and out of the shelter. Tom, one of the tallest, jumped and tipped some of the collecting water *accidentally* off the edge of the roof, then wanted to repeat this; we thought about how long it might take to collect a sufficient amount of water to pour off the top. (As adults, our roof design was flawed – a puddle was collecting in the middle of the roof, not running off a sloped roof.) Tom watched the water collecting in a puddle for a while, then ran off to fetch a long bough and asked for help to stand it in the middle of the den to create a 'pitched roof' (his explanation). We did this together, and water was now running off in two or three places. He said that we could collect it and went and found the bottles that were already full of drinking water; he tipped them out to collect 'real water'. Over the next 15–20 minutes, Tom compared how quickly the bottles filled off a pitched roof and, with the bough taken away, from the rain puddle tipped from the roof. He seemed satisfied with his goal, preferred the cascade rather than the gradual flow and could explain flow, pitch, depth and speed.

2 At the edge of the verandah outside the classroom, the guttering and down pipes from the flat roof let rainwater flow down a small grate; occasionally, the flow of water was too great and afforded puddle play. Mohammed was a child with an apparent vertical and connecting schema, always building, constructing, joining resources together, and he began to watch the water flow from the down pipe, showing concern that the playground would become flooded. He collected a bucket from the sandpit and held it underneath the pipe, collected the rain, took it to another drain, tipped it out, returned and repeated this activity for some time, before asking us if we had any more pipes. An idea had seemed to come to him to extend the pipework to 'carry the water' away from the small drain, to the one he had been using to tip out his own bucket. The next day it was not raining, but he asked for the crates, pipes and guttering to build a drainage and outflow system with water collected from the tap. Mohammed was investigating flow, drainage, volume and work efficiency.

Katz (1993) helps to explain what is happening in these encounters: 'The disposition to investigate may be thought of as inborn. When children's experiences support the manifestation of a disposition with appropriate scaffolding and environmental conditions, the disposition is likely to become robust.' These encounters demonstrate an effective community of learners: 'involving active learners and more skilled partners who provide leadership and guidance-learning involves transformation of participation in collaborative endeavour' (Rogoff *et al.*, 1996: 388). What is delightful here is that the active learners were both adults and children, as were the skilled partners. Tom was able to demonstrate an understanding of 'pitch' that the adults had not anticipated when hurriedly building a shelter in heavy rain. Mohammed sought assistance, but only to resource the structuring of his own activity.

As with the encounter involving Alice, becoming a community of learners and the notion of scaffolding are important for both children and adults, parents and practitioners. The time spent in the forest school with Otis in the puddle, then with one of his peers, Michael, was discussed with parents to see what their reflections were on the woodland sessions.

Encounter: Michael's mum

On 29 June, the weather was challenging, pretty torrential rain throughout, but I have noted that Michael has particularly enjoyed today. Often running and slipping, he has sprawled in the mud many times; his sleeves are wet, his face is covered in mud splash and he has giggled and shouted as the children have tried to catch water off the canopy.

Parents were called early that session as the children became quite cold.

Michael attended 5/6 sessions, and this evidence does not fully show the impact of forest school on his social and emotional development. It is only when reflecting with his mum, that we can see what this experience meant to him.

One of the leaders asked his mum: 'How do you think it has benefited Michael?' She said:

Freedom to do things without . . . worrying. He is sometimes not very good in large groups. Working in a small group has really helped him talk about forest school. He would go every single day. I think it has brought him on, brought on his confidence. He is more relaxed in preschool.

The leader responds: 'I've heard his voice in the forest more.'

Later his mum adds:

When we are out, he is always asking 'what tree is this?' He had a newt all week, let it crawl all over him, talked to it. Everything outdoors, he is interested. We've never built houses with sticks before, never done this before forest school. He knows nettles and dock leaves, telling his brother to hold his hands up high [brother is 2], he is choosing a lot more and will talk about forest school.

> Mum has seen a powerful impact upon Michael's voice, confidence, knowledge, well-being and autonomy and she really enjoyed telling us this. The leaders noted his speaking in the woods and they reflected that there had been concerns over his speech development. Confidence to speak in groups of children often hides the actual ability to converse and share dialogue, and it is wonderful to have been a part in his positive well-being in the woods. Sharing this with his mum was a very powerful event and will have encouraged her to become more engaged in the outdoors with her children.
>
> Michael, scored 5 (Laevers, 2005) each session for sustained involvement with others or on his own. His self-confidence developed from a 3 to 5 over the 5 weeks, with the added impact of others becoming more aware of his attributes as the weeks passed by.

Michael's mum, as with Alice's grandma, has been encouraged to participate in enjoyable, effective and reflective practice.

Communities of learners

In the encounter 'Annie with preschool', the final journal reflection is recorded: 'Jane, Annie, Lara, Penny, Sam and Charlie, members of a community of learners, sharing the responsibility of leading and following, actively listening, responding, asking and enjoying each other's learning, explanations and enjoyment within a child-led time frame'. Rogoff *et al.* concur, stating that:

> Schools organised as communities of learners are more self-consciously organised to promote children's learning, with more reflection and attention to the learning process. Organisation involves dynamic and complementary group relations among class members who learn to take responsibility for their contribution to their own learning and to the group's functioning. The discourse is often conversational, in the sense that people build on each other's ideas on a common topic. We argue that within the community of learners for adults under some circumstances to provide strong leadership or extensive explanations to assist the group, and for children under some circumstances to have primary responsibility.
>
> (1996: 397)

Guided participation is a joining in, not a taking over. It is about skilled engagement and an acknowledgement that, 'teaching can strengthen learning how to learn' (Edwards *et al.*, 1998: 83). Adjusted support that takes into account each child's willingness and ability to participate across a range of skills and attributes, to avoid unnecessary and devaluing interventions and enhancements, and that is both challenging and sensitive to the developing curiosity and resilience of children underpins the creation of possibilities for children to develop the many, active, characteristics of effective learning.

Provocations

- When did you last 'seek out a situation in which the child is about to see what the adult already sees' (Edwards *et al.*, 1998: 83), and what was your participation?

- Consider an observed interaction between an adult practitioner and child where the adult took charge. What happened next?

- What opportunities are afforded to children to work through problems and projects as a group of active participants?

- To what extent are the time frames of children guiding your participation?

- Reflect upon the last time you realised a child was a more skilled partner in your exchange and interaction? What was the interaction about, and what was your learning?

- Where do you like to spend your time working and playing with children, and what is your role in guiding your own and their participation?

- Do you recognise that you belong to a community of adult and child learners, and to what extent do you reflect upon and attend to your joint learning processes?

References

Brooker, L. and Edwards, S. (eds) (2010) *Engaging Play*. Maidenhead, UK: Open University Press.

Department for Education (2012) *Statutory Framework for the Early Years Foundation Stage (EYFS)*. Cheshire, UK: Department for Education.

Edwards, C., Gandini, L. and Forman, G. (1998) *The Hundred Languages of Children*, 2nd edn. Westport, CT: Ablex.

Engeström, Y., Miettinen, R. and Punamaki, R.-L. (eds) (1999) *Perspectives on Activity Theory*. New York: Cambridge University Press.

Hall, K., Murphy, P. and Soler, J. (eds) (2008) *Pedagogy and Practice: Culture and Identities*. Milton Keynes, UK: Open University Press.

Katz, L.G. (1993) *Dispositions: Definitions and Implications for Early Childhood Practice*. Urbana, IL: ERIC Clearinghouse on Elementary and Early Childhood Education [ED363454].

Laevers, F. (ed.) (2005) *Well-Being and Involvement in Care Settings: A Process-oriented Self-Evaluation*. Leuven, Belgium: Kind & Gezin and Research Centre for Experiential Education.

New Zealand Ministry of Education (1996) *Te Whāriki*. Wellington, New Zealand: Learning Media.

Ofsted (September 2013) *School Inspection Handbook*. Available at: www.ofsted.gov.uk/resources/120101 (accessed 24 October 2013).

Rogoff, B. (1990) *Apprenticeship in Thinking: Cognitive Development in Social Context*. Oxford, UK: Oxford University Press.

Rogoff, B., Matusov, E. and White, C. (1996) *Handbook of Education and Human Development*. Oxford, UK: Blackwell.

Rosen, M. (1989) *We're Going on a Bear Hunt*. London: Walker Books.

Stewart, N. (2011) *How Children Learn: The Characteristics of Effective Early Learning*. London: BAECE.

Waller, T., Whitmarsh, J. and Clarke, K. (eds) (2011) *Making Sense of Theory and Practice in Early Childhood: The Power of Ideas*. Maidenhead, UK: Open University Press.

Woods, A. (ed.) (2013) *Child-Initiated Play and Learning: Planning for Possibilities in the Early Years*. London: Routledge.

7

Sustained shared conversations

Victoria Brown

Bruner (1978: 255) urges us to, 'Believe that your child can understand more than he or she can say, and seek, above all, to communicate. To understand and to be understood.' This chapter builds on key ideas introduced in Chapter 1, where McEwan demonstrates, through her descriptions of early encounters between adults and babies, how human beings are pre-programmed to interact and share experiences with those who are familiar to them. She establishes the importance of ensuring rich and stimulating experiences and secure, loving, emotional relationships in order to nurture learning and development from the earliest moments of life. Goouch and Powell (2013: 57) state, 'the acquisition of language does not occur in a vacuum but rather in the company of interested others' and identify the need for 'endless opportunities to share conversations' (p. 60). Roberts (2010: 56) terms this 'companionable learning', which she sees as supporting children's well-being. This chapter takes these two key principles that can be seen to underpin effective communication encounters and suggests how adults can create a positive emotional and physical environment, where thinking is stimulated, sustained and shared with others through reciprocal interaction and conversation.

The development of thinking and language in children and babies has long been the focus of theorising and debate (Piaget, 1959; Bruner, 1983; Vygotsky, 1986), and the emergence of neuroscience in recent decades has contributed to and revolutionised thinking in this area. Babies are no longer viewed as being driven mainly by simple sensorimotor schemas, but as competent learners from birth. In the preface to their book, Gopnik, Meltzoff and Kuhl argue that babies and scientists have a lot in common:

> The new research shows that babies and young children know and learn more about the world than we could ever have imagined. They think, draw conclusions, make predictions, look for explanations, and even do

experiments. Scientists and children belong together because they are the best learners in the universe.

(Gopnik *et al.*, 2000: preface)

Since the large-scale, longitudinal Effective Provision of Pre-School Education (EPPE) Project (Sylva *et al.*, 2004) first introduced the term 'sustained shared thinking' into the common lexicon of early years practitioners, the concern to develop an effective pedagogy to support the development of thinking with children has gained prominence. Indeed, the emphasis on sustained shared thinking as a key feature of effective pedagogy is reflected in the *Teachers' Standards (Early Years)* (National College for Teaching and Leadership, 2013). Additionally, 'creating and thinking critically' is recognised as one of three enduring characteristics of effective learning, together with active learning, and play and exploration (Tickell, 2011a, 2011b; Department for Education (Department for Education), 2012; Early Education, 2012). Although the term 'sustained shared thinking' may be relatively new, the ideas behind it are not. They are heavily linked to the ideas of established theorists, such as Vygotsky's 'zone of proximal development' (ZPD) (1978), Wood *et al.*'s notion of 'scaffolding' (1976), Rogoff's theory of 'guided participation' (1998) and Alexander's 'dialogic teaching' (2004), many elements of which have been introduced in previous chapters.

The EPPE project defines sustained shared thinking as occurring:

when two or more individuals 'work together' in an intellectual way to solve a problem, clarify a concept, evaluate an activity, extend a narrative etc. Both parties must contribute to the thinking and it must develop and extend the understanding.

(Sylva *et al.*, 2004: 6)

The emphasis in the above definition is on extending children's cognitive learning and understanding and signals an expectation beyond general conversation. Owing to this emphasis on intellectual development, Sylva *et al.* (2004) state that it is more likely to occur in one-to-one interactions, with either an adult or a peer, and in focused group work; however, they note the strong potential of free-play activities to support sustained shared thinking and conclude that effective learning occurs where there is a balance between adults working to extend child-initiated play and teacher-initiated group work.

In discussing their research and coding of 'sustained shared thinking', Siraj-Blatchford (2009) describes how some interactions originally classified by researchers as 'dialogue' were subsequently designated as episodes of 'sustained shared thinking'. In order to demystify the term, it may be helpful to hold on to the idea of the origin of the term having its roots in dialogue and conversation. Vygotsky (1986) views language and thought as inseparable and considers that children who have a sound grasp of language also possess a sound ability to think. Engaging children in conversation, whether it involves sustained shared thinking or not, will nourish their language, communication and thinking. Conversation and interaction also give us a glimpse into the lives, experiences and interests of children; it allows us to connect. Wherever and whenever it happens, we need to make sure that we nurture, value and share it and, as Drummond (2003: 13) states, 'put our understanding to good use'.

Allen and Whalley (2010) argue, however, that there is confusion regarding the meaning of the term in practice. Conversations with practitioners in local primary schools and a range of early years settings and with undergraduate Initial Teacher Education students also demonstrate that this is largely the case, particularly for teachers working in Key Stage 1. In one primary school, a foundation stage practitioner, after initially expressing doubt over its meaning, said:

> When you talk about it like that, then yes, we do it. It is when you have a really good conversation, one which leaves you knowing a child better, one that makes you think 'they just learnt something'. We used to have a sustained shared thinking table; no one was sure how to use it. I can see now that it is not necessarily something you can plan to achieve at a specific time or place, but you can create the intention or the right conditions, an atmosphere rich in possibilities for thinking.

This chapter strives to deepen practitioners' understanding of the value of engaging in sustained shared thinking with children at different developmental stages and focuses on the role of *sustained shared interaction and conversation* as a key tool or context in nurturing and supporting this with children. Through offering informal and more structured encounters with children, at home and in a range of settings, this chapter considers children's different communication preferences: verbal and non-verbal. It is hoped to demonstrate that sustained shared thinking and interaction can occur in everyday moments, wherever and whenever adults are engaged with children, whether these moments are initiated by adults or by children or occur in informal or more formal contexts.

Progression in sustained shared interactions

Sustained shared thinking takes on different pedagogic forms, depending on the age of the child. It looks particularly different with babies and children under the age of 2 years. Siraj-Blatchford sees sustained shared thinking as part of a sequence of developmental progressions that extends into relationships in adulthood and becomes progressively more sophisticated:

There is an essential continuity between the playful collaborations of the nursery and the more formal collaborations between peers, and between teachers and pupils in school . . . In terms of competence, progression goes from mastering the very informal and strongly improvised sustained and shared interactions to more highly structured and much more formal sustained and shared interactions in adult life.

(2009: 6)

We start with an informal, playful, early interaction with a baby, before moving on to explore how thinking can develop in play and more formal educational encounters. In Chapter 1, McEwan states that the most important resource is an adult tuned in to respond appropriately to the child. This idea pervades the encounters, but is illustrated particularly aptly in this first encounter with a 5-month-old baby in a day nursery. The encounter also resonates with Trevarthen's 2004 work: through his close observation of 'proto conversations' between babies and their significant others, he proposed that babies often initiate and lead interactions that are then sustained by responsive and reciprocal adults, leading to episodes of 'mutual attunement', during which adults and babies have time to pay close attention to each other and initiate playful communication (cited by Goouch and Powell, 2013: 58).

Encounter: playing big eyes

The baby lies on her back looking up at the light dancing on the ceiling. As she sees the adult approaching with her bottle, she kicks and squeals excitedly, jumping her feet on the mattress. The adult puts the bottle down, leans over the pram, smiles and says warmly, 'Are you doing big eyes at me? Are you doing big eyes at me for your bottle?', while making her own eyes big and sparkly. She shakes her head playfully as she gently tickles the baby's tummy, all the time maintaining lively eye contact. She scoops the baby up, bringing her level with her own face and talking all the time in a sing-song voice. The baby puts her fingers in her carer's mouth. The carer pretends to eat the baby: 'I'm eating you up'. The carer transfers the baby to her hip and momentarily breaks eye contact to pick up the bottle and clear a space to sit down. The baby vocalises and bounces her body up and down, as if reminding her she is still there, getting more frantic and gesturing with her arms and hands as she sees the bottle. She is rewarded by the carer turning back to her; 'I'm here, I've got your bottle, it's coming'.

Here, the carer has established a close emotional connection with the baby. Reddy and Trevarthen argue that:

Engagement is how we gain psychological knowledge about others. If we want to know what a baby, an adult or, indeed, any animal feels or thinks, we have to engage with them, allowing ourselves to feel the sympathetic response that the other's actions and feelings invite.

(2004: 1)

They have had time to bond emotionally, to get to know each other and read each other's behaviour. Such a connection is indeed powerful and supports and motivates the carer in paying close attention to the baby. The baby is rewarded through receiving physical contact, affection and attention and is given rich opportunities to learn, through the social and communicative encounters she experiences and her interaction with the environment. Goouch and Powell (2013) suggest, however, that, although parents may be endlessly fascinated and tuned in to the needs of their child, practitioners may find it harder to establish an emotional attachment and may not be as intrinsically motivated to do so. They note that practitioners may also be more inhibited in their communication or lack confidence when being observed interacting with babies or engaging in 'pole-bridging' talk with older children. This will naturally impact on the quality of interactions, and the potential to engage in opportunities to develop language and thinking may be reduced.

When working with babies, very young or non-vocal children, it is vitally important that we as adults are tuned into their emerging needs and interests, as they may not express themselves verbally. Children show us their thinking most commonly and uninhibitedly in their freely chosen play. In their play, babies and children may ask questions and express their ideas and feelings with their bodies, through their facial expressions, sounds, body language, actions and gestures, as they interact and engage with the world around them using all of their senses. Movement can be seen as thought in action and, as such, allows thinking to become visible to observant others. Piaget (1983) was among the first to recognise organised and repeated behaviour patterns or cognitive structures in children under the age of 5, which are manifest through children's movement and actions. He termed this 'scheme of thought' or 'schemas of action' and saw thought as consisting of the internalisation of these schemas.

Questions, therefore, are not always asked with words; sometimes they are asked by gaze – for example, a wondering stare at a snail on the pavement. They may also be indicated by touch or by a child using sign language to enquire 'what is this?'. An alert practitioner will also notice a child who may be asking a question just by their facial expression and will comment, 'Umar, you look upset. Would you like a turn?'. A child lying down on their tummy so their eyes are on the same level as their action figure may be asking, 'What does he see? If I am him what would I see?'. Children may not ask the same questions we would ask as adults or questions that we could predict. If we take water play as an example, we might plan to ask key questions such as, 'Does the object float or sink?' or 'How many cups will fill the pot?'. Through our observations of children engaging in water play, however, their unspoken questions become apparent:

'How far can I make water travel?', 'Does water jump?', 'Can I make water jump by jumping?' (Listening and Questioning in the Early Years, 2006).

As well as through their gestures, sometimes we can literally hear children's thoughts and questions through their pole-bridging or self-talk, often heard as they describe their actions as they play and explore: 'Does this fit in here?', 'Can I jump off here?'. A verbal question may not always be phrased as a conventional question; it could be just a comment or a stated hypothesis – 'I jump!' or 'Rain makes puddles'. The practitioner's role is to be alert to these questions and to respond sensitively, 'in the moment', with their own comment – 'I love to jump in the puddles' – or to follow up the emerging ideas through providing resources that will encourage further exploration and investigation. Vygotsky (1978: 27) described such utterances as 'egocentric speech', which, he suggests, supports children in planning and guiding their own thinking and behaviour. He considered that this formed the basis of 'inner speech', where children begin to internalise their speech as thought. This process enables children to start to link words, actions and ideas together and underpins the development of critical thought (Winsler *et al.*, 2007). This process is supported by adults using a technique that is sometimes described as 'owling' – 'Observe, Wait, Listen' (Hanen, 2011). The use of this kind of speech, along with the use of gesture, can be seen in the following example.

Encounter: Eddie and the escalator

Eddie, aged 2 years 9 months, is at home in the front room and is twirling round, full of energy, concentration and purpose. He stops and says 'no, not dat', then makes diagonal arm movements, first with one arm and then with the other, crossing his arms upwards in front of him. He does this again and again while crouching and standing, crouching and standing. Mum has been watching him and wondering aloud, 'Eddie are you dancing? Are you dancing?'. He looks at her and carries on moving his arms. Mum says, 'up and down . . . up and down.' He determinedly continues to move his arms crossways diagonally upwards, while saying 'dis and dis', continuing to look directly at Mum. After a minute or two of repeated movement, Mum, recalling his fascination earlier that day, gradually realises what he is doing: 'Are you making the escalators from the shopping centre . . . the moving stairs?'. He replies with the upwards, diagonal gestures, 'One goes dis waim and dis waim . . . dis waim and dis waim'. He appears to be getting frustrated. Mum says, 'Did they both go up? Does one go down?'. Eddie tries again to represent the escalator. 'Clever boy! One goes up and the other goes down . . . this way and this way, and they cross over.' She copies his movements, 'Shall we make it with the Duplo?'.

Eddie is substituting an action in the place of the real object. He appears to be attempting to replicate the structure and movement of a visual image he holds of the escalator, representing it through his gestures and language. Through his exploration of movement, he is developing representational concepts and gaining access to the symbolic nature of language. While in the shopping centre, Eddie had been watching the escalators from his pushchair, and Mum had followed the line of his gaze but had not talked about it, other than saying 'escalator'. In retrospect, she can see that she missed an opportunity here to talk about the escalator 'in the moment', or to get Eddie out of the pushchair and ride on the escalator, but, through her active observation of activities and events that capture Eddie's attention, she is able to tune into his interest later in the day through his expressive movement play and help him to refine and develop his conceptual development, moving him towards different forms of representation through play. If this movement play had occurred anywhere else, or with anyone else, they would not have fully understood the context, and a learning moment might have been missed. This highlights the importance of two-way communication between home and setting to share observations and to try and make sense out of behaviours that might appear puzzling when taken out of context. Eddie's learning was captured in a 'learning story'; his model and the shopping-centre escalator were photographed and videoed, and a simple picture book was made and shared at bedtime and in the settings he attended. This not only provided Eddie with a visual record of his experiences that supported his ongoing conceptual development, but also, just as importantly, affirmed his sense of self and self-worth.

If parents and practitioners share their observations and stories of learning, there are benefits for all. Planning and provision can become more personalised, and individual curiosities and interests can be sustained and extended continuously, between home and setting. It also gives a focus to initiate discussion that can support transition between home and setting and can really help parents understand what their child has been doing during the day. A practitioner who shares an observation, 'Olivia wanted to wrap her apple up today as a present for someone', naturally leads the parent or carer to ask a follow-up question, 'Who did you want to give it to, Olivia?', genuinely valuing and responding to children's interests together.

Clearly, engaging with children in genuine opportunities for sustained shared conversation, in the home and while out and about, during daily routines and everyday experiences, is one way of stretching and challenging children's thinking. These do not need to be staged learning episodes; rather, they can develop from a question asked while feeding the ducks or shopping in the supermarket, or while observing the washing machine on spin cycle.

Although strictly outside the age range of this book, the following example of an older pupil engaging in a more formal episode of sustained shared thinking is offered, as it amply demonstrates the complex range of factors that can act to support the development of sustained shared conversations in the classroom. It also illustrates how sustained shared thinking can be developed and extended by using increasingly sophisticated and abstract scaffolding, and how it supports metacognition, which develops as children find it necessary to explain, describe and reason about their thinking and experiences with others (Siraj-Blatchford, 2009).

Encounter: Katya's developing perception of space

During an introductory lesson about the Earth in space, Katya is working with another pupil, and they are looking at a diagram of the structure of the Earth together and discussing it. Katya looks at it closely and asks of the teacher, 'I know I should know the answer to this . . . but are we standing on the inside or outside of the crust?'. The teacher responds with a gentle question, 'Where do you think we stand, Katya?'. 'Well, I think we stand on the inside of the Earth.' The teacher seeks to probe Katya's thinking further: 'Why do you think that Katya?'. 'Well, we must be on the inside because if you look at the diagram . . . if you stand on the outside and you look up then you would be able to see space.' The teacher pauses for a moment to take this in and then asks, 'OK, but when you look up at the sky at nighttime, what do you see?'. Realisation begins to dawn: 'oohhh!'. The teacher follows this up with an explicit response to ensure the connection is fully made: 'Well the stars and the night sky that you see . . . that is space'. Katya completes her moment of revelation and demonstrates her new understanding by expressing to her peer partner, 'So we stand on the outside then!'

Sylva *et al.* (2004) suggest that periods of shared thinking, which naturally involve open-ended questioning and modelling, are associated with better cognitive achievement in children. The value of skilled and responsive open-ended questioning can clearly be seen in the above encounter. Here, the teacher does not provide the answer; rather, he supports the pupil in questioning her own conceptual framework and arriving at her own conclusion. In research that extends and supports the findings of the EPPE project, Siraj-Blatchford and Manni (2008) found that only 5.5 per cent of questions asked by practitioners were open ended and, therefore, had potential to encourage sustained shared thinking or conversation.

If we deconstruct this encounter conversation further, we can see that this episode was able to occur owing to a combination of factors. First, the established learning environment was one where curiosity, thinking aloud, pondering and questioning were encouraged. The emotional environment was such that Katya felt safe to ask questions and to expose her unknowing or areas of confusion, safe in the knowledge that she would not be subject to ridicule or sarcasm; she knew her questions were actively listened to, valued by the teacher and taken seriously. This teacher made time, despite the pressures of teaching a large class, to engage in high-quality, one-to-one interaction that allowed him to assess levels of conceptual understanding and the working theories used by the child and to respond 'in the moment' to misconceptions. He allowed space and time for the child to unpick the mismatch in her own understanding, acting as a scaffold as she did so, allowing her to make connections and recognising the need to ensure his responses were explicit enough to lead to full understanding. Through the encounter, he was able to assess her current level of understanding and plan how to scaffold and support her conceptual development in subsequent sessions. Although the voice of the peer is not recorded in this encounter, there was strong evidence of collaborative learning: others around Katya were also helped by her questions and thinking. A community of learners and learning had been successfully established.

Children interacting and mediating meaning

Sustained shared conversations do not dwell solely in the domain of adult–child interaction. Children themselves can support and develop sustained shared conversation. Vygotsky (1978: 86) recognised this in his definition of the 'zone of proximal development', which is 'The distance between the actual developmental level as determined by independent problem solving and the level of potential development as determined through problem solving under adult guidance, or in collaboration with more capable peers'.

In the encounter between two children that follows, you can see that sometimes these conversations do not neatly resolve themselves, nor do they lead to enhanced conceptual development for both parties; they are, nonetheless, valuable opportunities for adults to observe and tune into a child's conceptual development, and for children themselves to explain and refine their own conceptual development in the company of their peers, often in play contexts. Here, the older child possesses a more sophisticated perception of 'baddies' than his younger play partner and tries to move the thinking of the younger child on through his ZPD; in doing so, he is forced to articulate and share his thinking.

Encounter: 'baddies think they are goodies really'

After a game of goodies and baddies, involving dressing up and a good deal of rough and tumble play, a 3-and-a-half-year-old child is heard to say: 'I'm a baddy!'. His older play partner (aged 5-and-a-half years) responds, 'No you wouldn't say that!'.

> Younger child: Why not? I am a baddy, I am really bad!
> Older child: If you really are a baddy, you wouldn't say, 'I'm a baddy'.
> Younger child: Well I am saying it . . . listen . . . [Shouts] I AM A BADDY!
> Older child: No, if you really are a baddy you wouldn't say that . . . because . . .

> Younger child: Why not? Why can't I say it?
> Older Child: . . . Because . . . because . . . [Pause] baddies think they are goodies really. They are bad . . . it is just like they think they are good but really they are bad but it isn't like they are pretending to be good . . .
> Younger child: But I'm not a goody! I'm a baddy! I'm not pretending to be good!
> Older child: You just need to think about it some more.
>
> In this final comment, the older child demonstrates his metacognitive awareness, his emerging understanding of the purpose of thinking and his experience of the language of thinking. Equally, the younger child feels sufficiently at ease to challenge the older child through his questions and to defend his own position.

Owing, perhaps, to the amount of time they spend together, siblings and peers can also be skilled at tuning in to each other's play, sometimes not even needing to communicate their intentions to each other. This is highlighted in the following encounter, where Mum has missed something that the older sibling has tuned into after hours of playing along with and interacting with his baby brother. Here, Isaac can be seen to act both as a partner in the development of shared thinking and as a mediator for meaning.

Encounter: 'lion says roar'

Mum is sitting on the sofa while Isaac (aged 42 months) and his brother Tyger (11 months) are playing with animals on the living-room floor. Isaac is making animal noises and moving the animals around, lining them up and making them fight or sleep. Tyger is watching and picking up the animals, holding them in both hands and occasionally putting them in his mouth or banging them on the floor. He too is vocalising. From time to time, he approaches Mum and shows her a lion and makes a noise, 'I-I-I-I'. She repeats the correct animal noise back to him, 'Lion says roar!'. After several turns of observing this interaction, Isaac intervenes: 'No, when he says I-I-I-I he is saying lion . . . he wants you to look at his lion and say lion, not make him roar'. [To his brother] 'Tyg, what do you want him to do now?' Tyger lays the lion down and says, 'Lally'. Isaac says, 'Is he asleep? Is he sleeping?'. He turns back to Mum and says, 'Sometimes he says 'Lally' and that means he wants the lion to lie down.'

As Mum's response is to take the opportunity to model the correct animal noises, without realising the significance of the noises Tyger is making to her, this encounter can be used to illustrate how easy it is, as adults, to introduce our own agendas, to seize the 'teachable moment' or simply to misunderstand a child's intent. Rose and Rogers (2012) put forward the notion of adults providing 'conceptual space' for children by listening carefully, allowing the child time and space to express and communicate their ideas and understanding. They recognise the challenge this may provide for practitioners who may possess a 'teacherly desire' to impart knowledge or introduce their own perspective, as in the following encounter.

Encounter: the spider

A trainee teacher is observed while engaging with a child in a reception class in a structured play activity. Children have been asked to use the play dough to make a mini beast that is the same on both sides. The child has made a model that has eight legs on the bottom and two legs on the top; she says, 'It is a spider'. The trainee, sitting across the corner of the table, looks at this and says, 'Mmm, how many legs does a spider have? . . . How many legs have you got on the bottom? . . . And how many have you got on the top? . . . Why don't you count them?'. The child looks at the model and counts as she has been asked. The teacher continues, 'Is your model the same on both sides?'. The child looks again at her model and replies 'Yes'. The teacher tries again, 'If you have more legs on the bottom . . . how can it be the same? A spider has the same number of legs on each side of its body.' The child looks at the teacher, picks up a ruler and uses the ruler to draw a vertical line through the mini beast, then she turns the dough mat towards the teacher. It is now apparent that the spider has four legs on each side of the ruler at the bottom. The child says, 'Those are two antennae at the top, not legs.'

In this encounter, the trainee teacher possibly learns more than the child. When asked what she had learned from the observation, the trainee said it served as a warning to always look at the world through the eyes of the child, to ask more tentative questions in order to find out about the child's agenda. She said that, in just one episode, she had learned to leave gaps in her questioning and allow children thinking time, so they had the time and opportunity to express their ideas.

Finding the right balance

Sylva *et al.* (2004) assert that effective pedagogy involves a balance of 'potentially instructive' teacher-initiated and child-initiated group work and play activities. Practitioners are aware, however, of the tensions in achieving this pedagogical balance in practice, where they face the challenge of weighing their inclination and requirement to 'teach' against the child's right and inclination to play. On top of this, the nature of the practitioner's involvement in children's play can also be seen to be problematic.

The role of the adult in acting to guide and support learning for children is readily accepted and can be seen in the theories of Vygotsky, Bruner and Rogoff. For Vygotsky (1978), 'more capable' adults or peers act to guide the child to build on what they already know. Bruner (1983) and Rogoff (1990) see the learning relationship in terms of an apprenticeship between experienced learner and novice. For Bruner, the expert is seen to take a leading role in 'scaffolding' the learning. Rogoff (1990, 1998) proposes an alternative to the dichotomy of teacher as instructor or teacher as facilitator, in the form of learning through 'guided participation', where children and adults work together in shared endeavour to construct meaning (for a full discussion of this, see Chapter 6).

The role of the adult in play is not so clear cut; adults may not always be readily accepted or tolerated in play situations. Hadley (2002), drawing on Csíkszentmihályi's (1990) theory, sees adults as being positioned either outside or inside the process and flow of children's play, but asserts both as part of the teacher's repertoire. Play is variously reconceptualised in the current literature as *playful structure* (Walsh *et al.*, 2011) or *playful pedagogies* (Moyles, 2010), with practitioners adopting a range of integrated pedagogies (Wood, 2013), acting as co-players and bringing playfulness to their teaching and engaging with children in episodes of 'sustained shared playing' (Wood and Attfield, 2005: 106).

Fleer (2010) discusses Vygotsky's theory of conceptual development (1987), where children are seen to develop their 'everyday' concepts through their everyday interactions, but require teaching or instruction in order to build more formal, abstract, 'scientific' concepts. Influenced by this theory, Fleer recognises the possibilities for conceptual development ensuing from the adult framing of play activities in order to support the development of specific concepts: for example, introducing ice cubes to water play with the intent to support children's conceptual development of changing state. She suggests that children may more readily accept adult involvement in this type of encounter rather than in their free play; however, care must be taken to ensure that such adult-framed experiences are both engaging and meaningful to children.

The following encounter, documented by the trainee in a further session, is presented as a positive example of her learning about scaffolding and guiding sustained shared thinking, while engaging playfully with a child in the outside area.

Encounter: who wants chips?

Evee is playing shops in the den under the climbing equipment. She shouts out the window, 'Anybody want chips?'. I [the trainee] say, 'I would like some chips please, Miss.' Evee passes me a handful of bark chips. 'Do you have any ketchup Evee? Lovely, thank you. How much is that?' I pretend to give Evee the 'money'. Evee responds, 'No! I give you the money!' I respond by looking puzzled and saying 'Oh?'

and pausing. Evee thinks and says, 'The shop man gives my Mum the money.' I reply, 'If I have chips from your shop I think I should give you some money for them?' Evee says, 'You give me the money and then I give it back to you like at the shop.' I think and then reply, 'He must have been giving your mummy the change. Here's my money to pay you for the delicious chips. Thank you. Oh! I have given you too much. Please can you give me some back as my change?' Later Evee is observed saying to another child, 'You ate my chips, give me the money now and then I give it back to you . . . here you go, this is your change'.

The shared nature of the thinking that has taken place in these encounters, such as this between adult and child or between children, needs highlighting; to achieve a genuine shared interaction, practitioners need to work to guide and challenge children to think in deeper ways without intruding too heavily on children's play agendas or disturbing the child's train of thought. Such interaction requires a depth of skill, awareness and sensitivity in the adult. Purdon (2013: 1) emphasises the reciprocal nature of interactions when she states that sustained shared thinking, 'is neither solely teacher directed nor solely child-initiated. The very fact that it is "shared" indicates that the thinking and interaction between the two participants is apportioned'.

This suggests the need for joint engagement and involvement and implies relationships of equity and trust in learning and teaching. Although both parties must be involved in the thinking, there does not necessarily need to be equal contribution to the conversation, but there does need to be reciprocity in the interaction (Rose and Rogers, 2012). Jordan (2009: 43) sees such shared episodes as involving *co-construction*, which she sees as requiring participants to work together to share and create meaning. She reiterates, 'Studying meaning requires teachers and children to make sense of the world, interpreting and understanding activities and observations as they interact with each other.'

This co-construction of learning is resonant with the approaches used in the municipal preschools and infant–toddler centres of Reggio Emilia, which have been heavily influenced by social constructivist theories and which hold a construct of the child as *'rich in potential, strong, powerful, competent'* (Malaguzzi 1993: 10). This construct is central to their ideology and, through its framing of children as capable citizens in their own right, redresses the balance of power in relationships between teachers and learners (MacNaughton and Williams, 2009) and recognises children as powerful agents in their own learning (Anning, 2009).

This image is reflected in practice in Reggio settings, where practitioners act to co-construct learning in dialogue, with children as collaborative partners (Rinaldi, 2006). Through its respectful ethos, the Reggio approach encapsulates and preserves children's right to be heard (Moran, 2013), inclusively empowering child 'voice' through encouraging children to express their thoughts and ideas through their 'hundred languages'. Through representing their ideas in various forms, children refine and develop their conceptual awareness, as they translate their understanding by drawing, dancing, modelling and using sound, gesture, technology or story to express their ideas. The adult role is to provide resources and support in this process and to be aware of alternative possibilities. In order to achieve such an approach, practitioners need, not just sound pedagogic knowledge, but also strong relational knowledge and understanding, in order to respond to, interact and engage with children in respectful and authentic ways.

Rinaldi (2006) discusses the importance of developing 'a pedagogy of listening', which she sees as requiring a sense of openness to the unexpected. We need to recognise that learning never ends and position ourselves as learners (May *et al.*, 2006), both in finding out about the children in our care and in modelling curiosity. As adults, we need to be aware of the two-way nature of conversation and become genuine in our listening: we must make sure that we pay good attention to what children have to say, to make them feel listened to. This is not always easy in a busy setting; however, it is not enough to just appear interested: we need to *be* interested in what they have to say – children know when we are not really listening to them. If we are able to take time to truly listen, then we can gain fascinating glimpses into the lives, thoughts and perspectives of children, leading to greater mutual understanding and more authentic involvement.

Adults who promote talking and thinking

Opportunities to talk and think together should be part of the fabric of the child's daily experiences. Children need rich opportunities, indoors and outside, which provoke their interest and fascination, stimulate their drive for discovery and fire their imagination, giving them something to talk about, to question and ponder. Open-ended and natural materials are particularly useful for this – they are endlessly variable and unique and possess many possibilities. Such an environment promotes 'possibility thinking' (Craft, 2002, 2011a) and involves children in making a shift in their thinking from 'what is' to 'what might be' (Craft *et al.*, 2012: 49). Possibility thinking is also rich in potential for developing children's imaginative abilities, allowing them to take on other roles and try out seeing the world from different standpoints (Craft, 2011b), developing their awareness of different perspectives in thinking.

Adults can model the language of thinking or engage in 'thinking talk'. This can be as simple as using the word *thinking*, more frequently and in context with children – for example, 'Good thinking, Charlie' or 'Shall I tell you what I am thinking?'. In settings where the use of 'talk partners' is familiar, this pairing can be adapted to introduce 'thinking partners', who think together about a problem or issue and suggest solutions. Some settings, adopting the ideas of De Bono (2000), ask children to physically show they are thinking or getting ready to think, by *'putting on their thinking caps'*. Other settings use examples from the programme Philosophy4Children.

> Philosophy for Children offers a way to open up children's learning through enquiry and the exploration of ideas. Children learn that their ideas have value, and that the ideas of other children have value too. Through Philosophy for Children they realise that they don't always have to be right, but they gain the confidence to ask questions and learn through discussion.
> (www.philosophy4children.co.uk)

Many use symbols and signing to encourage children to stop, listen, share, talk and think. These physical and visual reminders are good prompts for all children. Children who are exposed to this kind of talk will often begin to ask themselves and others similar questions and so take on the thinking process for themselves.

Routines in the day can be adapted to provide time over the course of the day for short bursts of planning, reflection and review with children, all of which support the development of children's thinking skills. Wiltshire (2012), in discussing the high-scope model of plan–do–review, suggests that a range of active approaches can be adopted, including children acting out and taking 'tours' of the environment, or using objects of reference to support recall and reflection. Informal discussions of activities, paintings, drawing and models can all be good contexts to support sustained shared thinking. Katz (2008) asserts that questions must be serious and respectful and should not ask children to repeat what you already know. She suggests that asking questions such as 'Is your drawing as complete as you want it to be?' will encourage children to develop lifelong dispositions to think and evaluate.

Many settings capture the questions children have at the start of a new theme or topic; these questions can then become the focus for planning with children and also provide a useful record for practitioners and children to refer back to, during and at the conclusion of the project or theme, and an opportunity to model thinking and involve children in opportunities for thinking and dialogue about learning.

Philosophical approaches are popular in some settings. One setting provides a question book that is used to log the questions children are asking at home and school and affords a fascinating insight into their various worlds, ideas and experiences. Another setting has a question 'trail' snaking around the room at child height, where any questions arising in school or at home can be stuck up, and anyone can respond to them. Parents were particularly keen to support children in researching 'where are the seeds in a pineapple?', to the extent that this became the focus of activity for the next few weeks and involved cutting, observing and handling fruit, Internet research and correspondence with the Royal Botanic Gardens at Kew.

Of course, we cannot ignore the possibilities that exist for thinking in the sharing of stories. Questions arise naturally in the reading and telling of stories: 'Why did the gingerbread man want to run away?', 'Do burglars always wear stripy t-shirts?'. Gussin-Paley (1986, 1990) demonstrates how children's stories, scribed by adults, can be dramatised, the decision-making that goes into deciding 'who will play the part of the aeroplane?', and the shared meaning making that can occur as children listen and watch their stories come to life.

This chapter has offered a range of factors and approaches to consider when initiating and responding to children in episodes of sustained shared interaction and conversation; however, it is important to remember that the most important thing is to relax, trust your instincts and have a go. 'There is no set of rules of how to talk to a child that can even approach what you unconsciously know. If you concentrate on communicating, everything else will follow' (Bruner, 1978: 255).

After focusing on sustained shared interaction in her professional practice, one practitioner commented:

> I'm getting better at it each time. I find the children's individual approaches utterly absorbing, to the extent I have been talking to other colleagues and to parents about little things that happened. All parents really want to know is that someone has noticed things about their child, what they know, who they play with, it gives them confidence in the setting.

This final comment emphasises the need for practitioners themselves to engage in opportunities for sustained shared *professional* dialogue and debate and, in doing so, gain understanding about their children to support the development of reflective practice. This practitioner has recognised the value of *knowing* the children, and this will be discussed further in the final chapter; knowing the children appears to ensure that we fully appreciate children's unique characteristics of effective learning.

Provocations

- *Te Whāriki* (New Zealand Ministry of Education, 1996: 84) poses the following question for practitioners to reflect on: 'What kind of role do adults have when children are playing, and how do these roles promote children's learning?'.

- Are you accepted as a play partner? Do children carry on their play when you join in or observe? Are your adult-initiated encounters playful or 'teacherful?'

- Are you a good listener? How do you know?

- Do you communicate with *all* children in your setting? Are there certain children who gain more attention? Are there certain children you find it easier to communicate with?

- How much conceptual space do you leave for children to express themselves and their ideas?

- Which kinds of question proliferate in your setting? You may wish to record samples of your dialogue.

- Does the learning environment, inside and outside, provoke children's curiosity and actively promote enquiry and exploratory play?

References

Alexander, R. (2004) *Towards Dialogic Teaching: Rethinking Classroom Talk*. York, UK: Dialogos.

Allen, S. and Whalley, M.E. (2010) *Supporting Pedagogy and Practice in Early Years Settings*. Exeter, UK: Learning Matters.

Anning, A. (2009) The co-construction of an early childhood curriculum. In Anning, A., Cullen, J. and Fleer, M. (eds) *Early Childhood Education: Society and Culture*. London: Sage, pp. 67–80.

Bruner, J.S. (1978) The Role of Dialogue in Language Acquisition. Inaugural lecture of the Max-Planck-Gesellschaft, Projektgruppe fur Psycholinguistik. Available online at: http://down load.springer.com/static/pdf/583/bbm%253A978-3-642-67155-5%252F1.pdf?auth66= 1400081901_5aeab1263c23e44af403e0a85b51c6cc&ext=.pdf (accessed 18 January 2014).

Bruner, J.S. (1983) *Child's Talk: Learning to Use Language*. New York: Norton.

Craft, A. (2002) *Creativity and Early Years Education: A Lifewide Foundation*. London: Continuum.

Craft, A. (2011a) Creativity and early years settings. In Paige-Smith, A. and Craft, A. (eds) *Developing Reflective Practice in the Early Years*. Buckingham, UK: Open University Press, pp. 87–100.

Craft, A. (2011b) The possibilities are endless! *Teach Nursery* 1(3): 49–50.

Craft, A., McConnon, L. and Matthews, A. (2012) Child-initiated play and professional creativity: Enabling four-year-olds' possibility thinking. *Thinking Skills and Creativity* 7: 48–61.

Csíkszentmihályi, M. (1990) *Flow: The Psychology of Optimal Experience*. New York: HarperCollins.

De Bono E. (2000) *Six Thinking Hats*. London: Penguin.

Department for Education (2012) *Statutory Framework for the Early Years Foundation Stage (EYFS)*. Runcorn, UK: Department for Education.

Drummond, M. (2003) *Assessing Children's Learning*. London: David Fulton.

Early Education (2012) *Development Matters in the Early Years Foundation Stage (EYFS)*. London: Early Education.

Fleer, M. (2010) *Early Learning and Development: Cultural–Historical Concepts in Play*. Cambridge, UK: Cambridge University Press.

Goouch, K. and Powell, S. (2013) *The Baby Room. Principles, Policy and Practice*. Maidenhead, UK: Open University Press.

Gopnik, A., Meltzoff, A.N. and Kuhl, P.K. (2000) *The Scientist in the Crib. What Early Learning Tells Us About the Mind*. New York: HarperCollins.

Gussin-Paley, V. (1986) On listening to what the children say. *Harvard Educational Review* 56(2): 122–32.

Gussin-Paley, V. (1990) *The Boy Who Would Be a Helicopter. The Uses of Storytelling in the Classroom.* New York: Cambridge, MA: Harvard University Press.

Hadley, E. (2002) Playful disruptions. *Early Years: An International Research Journal* 22(1): 9–17.

Hanen (2011) OWL to let your child lead. Hanen Early Language Program. Available online at: www.hanen.org/Images-for-public-site/Links—Sample-PDFs/ITTTp17-18S.aspx (accessed 18 January 2014).

Jordan, B. (2009) Scaffolding learning and co-constructing understandings. In Anning, A., Cullen, J. and Fleer, M. (eds) *Early Childhood Education: Society and Culture.* London: Sage, pp. 39–53.

Katz, L. (2008) Always respect the learner. *Early Years Educator* 10(1): 8.

Listening and Questioning in the Early Years (2006) *Early Years Workshop Series.* Teachers TV television programme. Available online at: www.tes.co.uk/teaching-resource/Teachers-TV-Listening-and-Questioning-in-EY-6083778/ (accessed 27 December 2013).

MacNaughton, G. and Williams, G. (2009) *Teaching Young Children Choices in Theory and Practice,* 2nd edn. Maidenhead, UK: Open University Press.

Malaguzzi, L. (1993) For an education based on relationships. *Young Children* 49(1): 9–12.

May, P., Ashford, E. and Bottle, G. (2006) *Sound Beginnings: Learning and Development in the Early Years.* London: Routledge.

Moran, M. (2013) Exploring the possibilities of children's voice. In Woods, A. (ed.) *Child-Initiated Play and Learning: Planning for Possibilities in the Early Years.* Abingdon, UK: Routledge, pp. 37–50.

Moyles, J. (2010) Practitioner reflection on play and playful pedagogies. In Moyles, J., *Thinking about Play.* Buckingham, UK: Open University Press, pp. 13–30.

National College for Teaching and Leadership (2013) *Teachers' Standards (Early Years).* Available online at: www.gov.uk/government/publications/early-years-teachers-standards (accessed 18 January 2014).

New Zealand Ministry of Education (1996). *Te Whāriki. Te whāriki mātauranga mō ngā mokopuna o Aotearoa. Early Childhood Curriculum.* Wellington, New Zealand: Learning Media.

Piaget, J. (1959) *The Language and Thought of the Child,* 3rd edn. London: Routledge & Kegan Paul.

Piaget, J. (1983) Piaget's theory. In Mussen, P. (ed.) *Handbook of Child Psychology,* 4th edn. Vol. 1. New York: Wiley.

Purdon, A. (2013) An exploration of practitioners' perspectives of promoting sustained shared thinking in an early childhood setting. A case study. Available online at: www.tactyc.org.uk/pdfs/2013-conf-Purdon.pdf (accessed 18 January 2014).

Reddy, V. and Trevarthen, C. (2004) What we learn about babies from engaging their emotions. *Zero to Three* 24(3): 9–15.

Rinaldi, C. (2006) *In Dialogue With Reggio Emilia: Listening, Researching and Learning.* London: Routledge.

Roberts, R. (2010) *Wellbeing From Birth.* London: Sage.

Rogoff, B. (1990) *Apprenticeship in Thinking: Cognitive Development in Social Context.* New York: Oxford University Press.

Rogoff, B. (1998) Cognition as a collaborative process. In Damon, W. (series ed.) and Kuhn, D. and Siegler, R.S. (vol. eds) *Handbook of Child Psychology: Cognition, Perception, and Language,* 5th edn. New York: Wiley, pp. 679–744.

Rose, J. and Rogers, S. (2012) *The Role of the Adult in Early Years Settings.* Maidenhead, UK: Open University Press.

Siraj-Blatchford, I. (2009) Conceptualising progression in the pedagogy of play and sustained shared thinking in early childhood education: A Vygotskian perspective. *Educational and Child Psychology* 26(2): 77–89.

Siraj-Blatchford, I. and Manni, L. (2008) 'Would you like to tidy up now?' An analysis of adult questioning in the English Foundation Stage. *Early Years: An International Research Journal* 28(1): 5–22.

Sylva, K., Melhuish, E., Sammons, P., Siraj-Blatchford, I. and Taggart, B. (2004) *The Effective Provision of Pre-school Education (EPPE) Project: Final Report.* London: DfES and Institute of Education, University of London.

Tickell, D.C. (2011a) *The Early Years: Foundation for Life, Health and Learning. An Independent Report on the Early Years Foundation Stage to Her Majesty's Government.* Available online at: www.education.gov.uk/tickellreview (accessed 29 July 2011).

Tickell, D.C. (2011b) *The Early Years Foundation Stage (EFYS) review. Report on the evidence.* Available online at: www.education.gov.uk/tickellreview (accessed 29 July 2011).

Vygotsky, L.S. (1978) *Mind and Society: The Development of Higher Mental Process.* Cambridge, MA: Harvard University Press.

Vygotsky, L.S. (1986) *Thought and Language* (newly revised and edited by A. Kozulin). Cambridge, MA: MIT.

Vygotsky, L.S. (1987) Thinking and speech. In Vygotsky, L.S. *The Collected Works of L.S. Vygotsky, Vol. 1, Problems of General Psychology* (R.W. Rieber and A.S. Carton (eds), N. Minick (trans.)). New York: Plenum Press. pp. 39–285.

Walsh, G., Sproule, L., McGuinness, C. and Trew, K. (2011) Playful structure: a novel image of early years pedagogy for primary school classrooms. *Early Years: An International Research Journal* 32(2): 107–19.

Winsler, A., Manfra, L. and Diaz, R.M. (2007) 'Should I let them talk?' Private speech and task performance among preschool children with and without behavior problems. *Early Childhood Research Quarterly* 22: 215–31.

Wiltshire, M. (2012) *Understanding the High Scope Approach: Early Years Education in Practice.* London: David Fulton.

Wood, D., Bruner, J. and Ross, G. (1976) The role of tutoring in problem solving. *Journal of Child Psychology and Psychiatry* 17(2): 89–100.

Wood, E. (2013) *Play, Learning and the Early Childhood Curriculum*, 3rd edn. London: Sage.

Wood, E. and Attfield, J. (2005) *Play, Learning and the Early Childhood Curriculum*, 2nd edn. London: Sage.

8

Capturing the possibilities

Moira Moran

This final chapter will explore the familiar spiral of observation, assessment and planning in the context of the new requirement on early years practitioners to report on characteristics of effective learning. This requirement to report on characteristics affords settings an opportunity to reflect on values and pedagogy and to consider the construct of the child (Rinaldi, in Brown, 2013).

Previous chapters have explored the characteristics of children's effective learning and the pedagogic characteristics of the environments and relationships that enable a learning that has its beginnings with the child (child initiated) and its middle and ending with the child (child led). They have discussed the notion of 'purposeful play', where the purpose and process of learning are the child's and result in a learning that can be deep and meaningful to the child. They have also discussed the adult role as co-constructor, co-learner, more knowledgeable other, guide and so much more.

McEwan helps us to discover the exploratory learning processes of the youngest child, and Hall demonstrates the competencies of all our children. Gripton's chapter proposes that higher-order thinking skills can be developed by all children and employed in any situation, and are not the domain of older children only. Wardle and Vesty turn our attention to the importance of positive relationships that support a child's developing sense of self, starting with the practitioner's knowledge of the child, building up the child's trusting relationship and resulting in the child's ability to fly in thinking and puzzling and knowing (Podmore *et al.*, 2001). Woods extends this idea of children learning and developing their thinking in partnership with people, to include the places and things through which children explore and develop in an enabling environment, indoors and out. She introduces us to Sonnyboy's frustration when his learning is interrupted by adults just when he gets to the interesting bit – an issue that is picked up and explored further in Brown's chapter, which advocates, rather, that adults tune in to what is important to children, in order to be able to join them as play partners and co-constructors.

Woven into each of these chapters, linking them to each other like the threads in a web, and linking them to the practitioner at the centre, like the spokes of a wheel, are the encounters with children. Each of these encounters is designed to illustrate a point and to bring it to life for you, the reader. Importantly, each of these encounters is an observation, made by the author or a colleague, and carefully reflected on, discussed, unpicked and assessed, in order to try to understand what the child is telling us about the learning that is taking place. Consequently, it is important to consider that, although observation and assessment are the subject of this final chapter, it is by no means the last thing to think about or do; rather, it permeates everything we think about and do with the children in our care, so that we can best provide for them. As Drummond (1993: 13) wrote, 'Assessment is the way in which in our everyday practice, we observe children's learning, strive to understand it, and then put our understanding to good use.'

How could we observe?

All settings and all practitioners are familiar with observation of children to inform assessment and planning for future provision. Often, these observations focus on what children have learned. Practitioners want to know if the children count accurately, if they can form letters correctly, if they have understood our teaching on floating and sinking, or how to use a knife safely. All of these assessments are important, indeed they are required in order to inform many different audiences: themselves, the children, the parents, the head or manager, the early years foundation stage profile (EYFSP), the local authority and Ofsted, to name a few.

Katz (1993: 1) suggests that practitioners should be aware of, and planning for, 'at least four types of learning goals, those related to knowledge, skills, dispositions, and feelings'. She proposes that knowledge, skills and feelings are foregrounded in the educational goals of most practitioners and continues, 'However, dispositions are seldom included, although they are often implied by the inclusion of attitudes (e.g., attitudes toward learning) as goals' (ibid.: 1).

Malaguzzi (1998: 82), in conversation with Gandini, said, 'Stand aside for a while and leave room for learning, observe carefully what children do, and then, if you have understood well, perhaps teaching will be different from before'. He has put the emphasis on the process of the child's learning and doing, rather than the product. He is advocating an additional, different, but complementary type of observation that must then be puzzled over and discussed, so that understanding can inform what effective teaching happens next.

Observing the characteristics of children's learning can require a new lens through which to observe *how* children learn, rather than *what* they learn, to look at what we are seeing rather than to see what we are looking for. It is useful here to revisit Nutbrown, who wrote:

> Children approach their learning with wide eyes and open minds, so their educators too need wide eyes and open minds to see clearly and to understand what they see. If educators are blinkered, having tunnel vision, they may not have the full picture – so it's not simply a case of understanding what is seen but it is crucial to *see* what is *really happening* and not what adults sometimes suppose to be happening. Children and the things they do need to be seen in the whole context and adults working with them must be open to seeing what *exists* not what their professional mind tells them they *should* see. Educators need wide eyes too, to guard against stereotypes and to combat prejudices about capabilities of children based on such factors as their gender, race, language, culture or disability.
>
> (Nutbrown, 1996: 45)

Hall provides a considerable amplification of this last idea in Chapter 2.

The practitioner with eyes and mind open to a wide range of possibilities, rather than only focused upon predetermined specifics, will gather a wealth of detail to contribute to her picture of the child. As Eisner (1985, in Blenkin and Kelly, 1992: 7) wrote, 'Our nets determine what we catch'. Imagining our observations and assessments as nets, if we decide that we only want to catch whales with our nets, then we will miss all the little sardines swimming by.

Theoretical perspectives on observing a child's development

For many practitioners, using wide eyes and open minds to observe and assess is accustomed practice. Certainly, theorists of child development and pioneers of approaches to children's learning have provided underpinning rationales and frameworks for this approach.

Vygotsky (1978) and Bruner (1976, in Wood *et al.*, 1976) saw learning as a scaffolded process of social construction, in which children learn from more knowledgeable others, adult and peers. Vygotsky's 'zone of proximal development' can be seen as a social system co-constructed by the child as learner and the adult or peer as teacher offering scaffolding support. Rogoff (2003) presents learning as the child's guided participation in the experiences and activities of her culture and community and is examined in Woods' chapter. Karlsdóttir and Garðarsdóttir (2010: 256) describe learning as:

the process of adopting knowledge, skills, understanding and social competence in co-construction with others by participating in a social context. As a social construction, learning involves being able to 'read' a setting, to communicate in it and to understand different roles, rules and connections associated with it.

(2010: 256)

Encounter: mealtime as a social occasion

It is mealtime, and Max (4 months) is in his bouncy chair, next to the table where everyone else is gathering to eat. He is happy enough, listening to the chatter and joining in from his position on the floor. But, in his low position, he is somewhat excluded from the group, unable to see all the faces or to be seen by the whole group. After some minutes, his mood shows signs of changing: he wriggles in his chair, arches his back, and his babbling is interspersed with little cries. So, his carer picks him up and sits him on her knee while she eats. Immediately, Max cheers up again. He looks from person to person as they talk. He kicks his little legs in excitement when the conversation is addressed to him. He watches intently and with interest as they eat and interact. Max is a really social baby.

From this brief observation of Max at mealtime, we learn about his social development, his communication skills, his developing motor control and his interest in the world, but Max is also telling us much about the ways in which he is making sense of the world around him and about what is important to him. At 4 months, he is already 'reading' the social situation of mealtime within his culture, understanding and asserting his role in the community, and joining competently and with pleasure in the conventions of communication. His observant practitioner enables his full participation in the social context and supports his learning by her timely response to his changing communications. She is helping him to enjoy his involvement in the life of the setting. This encounter returns us to McEwan's careful observations in Chapter 1.

Being perceptive to the nuances of a baby's actions, being reflective on what that tells us and being responsive to them are skills that can demand much of the early years practitioner. Powell and Goouch (2012: 5) advocate 'mindful care', particularly in the care of babies, 'what [they] describe as "authentic professionalism"; the idea of professionalism which comes from within, from who we are, our levels of commitment, our expertise and experience'.

Encounter: amazing baby!

During a tutorial back at university, Hayley, a student, discussed her learning journey on placement in the baby room. 'At first my observations were really short. I wrote things like, "Baby S was sitting on the mat. She looked at the things in the basket and picked some of them up"'. Hayley smiles, a little sheepishly.

> I just didn't know what I was looking at. But the longer I spent in the baby room, and the more I got to know S and the practitioners, the more detailed my observations got. S is great, she really knows what she wants and she concentrates for AGES on the littlest thing, really exploring it; she turns it round and sucks it, and shows it to K (key person) to look at, then has another look. And K is so tuned in to S, they are a real team. At first I thought the baby room might be difficult to do observations, I thought babies don't really DO much, but she does. She's amazing!

Hayley is starting out on her career; she will build up her expertise and experience, but already she is demonstrating 'professionalism within' and a level of commitment to the child, fed by her receptivity to how Baby S is learning and her awareness of the social aspect of children's learning, that, 'even babies who can't talk yet are naturally cultural beings' (Gopnik *et al.*, 1999: 35). She is already demonstrating that she meets, albeit perhaps unknowingly, the requirements identified in the *Te Whāriki* curriculum (New Zealand Ministry of Education, 1996: 22) for the care of the youngest children:

> The care of infants is specialised and is neither a scaled-down three- or four-year-old programme nor a baby-sitting arrangement. Any programme catering for infants must provide one-to-one responsive interactions (those in which caregivers follow the child's lead), an adult who is consistently responsible for, and available to, each infant . . . [and] sociable, loving, and physically responsive adults who can tune in to an infant's needs.

She is also aware of the impact her developing skills of observation and reflection have had on her ability to meet those requirements.

Piaget's concept of schematic learning, defined by Athey (1990: 37) as, 'a pattern of repeatable behaviour into which experiences are assimilated and that are gradually coordinated', provides us with a different lens through which to observe young children at all stages of development. Children repeat, revisit, refine and review their experiences and environments in their unstoppable urge and quest to make sense of their world. They explore their interests, fascinations, passions and, at times, obsessions, from every angle and in every context, and project their current understanding on to new experiences.

Encounter: busy boy

Gabe is very busy. He is currently deeply involved in exploring a rotational schema. He likes to walk along beside the settee, rolling his cars, so that he can watch the wheels go round at eye height. He commentates on his practitioner's bracelet, which goes 'round and round' her arm, as the beads go 'round and round' too. His favourite story is 'The very hungry caterpillar' and he enjoys putting his finger in the round holes in the pages. His new exploration is of the small plastic 'dinosaur eggs' from his recent birthday party. Again and again he hides them and collects them in his bucket. He takes them apart and, by looking carefully at the round holes of the two halves, fits them back together with unerring accuracy, leading him to sort them by size, his first classification of objects by this criterion.

A casual observer of Gabe may see very little in the way of purposeful play, may see him darting from experience to experience and may be frustrated by his ignoring planned activities and resources provided in favour of some empty plastic eggs, which cost pence from the Pound Shop. However, a more informed and receptive practitioner would observe him not flitting from content to content of activity, but fitting together his forms of thinking through meaningful explorations of rotation and roundness, 'by an almost invisible thread of thinking' (Nutbrown, 1999: 48). In those words, 'almost invisible', Nutbrown herself alludes to the observational skill required of the practitioner, the extent of her knowledge of the child and her receptivity to what she is seeing.

Different ways of seeing

Wardle and Vesty have already discussed the work of Laevers (2005) in Chapter 4. It is exactly the characteristics of effective learning that Laevers enables to be assessed through use of his scales of well-being and involvement – involvement in particular. Laevers names his publication, *A Process-oriented Self-evaluation*. Through observations of 'the process within the child and how children are doing' (ibid.: 6), he is advocating observation of *how* the child is learning. He proposes that an analysis of the child's levels of well-being and involvement enables practitioners to evaluate how well the setting is providing for the individual child and 'how they are doing'. This then leads practitioners to, 'learn to take the perspective of the child in their approach and because of this to create optimal conditions for the social–emotional and cognitive development' (ibid.: 3). An increasing number of settings are using Laevers' observation scales to add to and support their spiral of observation, assessment and planning and, importantly, to include the sometimes forgotten aspect of observation that is reflective self-evaluation.

Donaldson (2006: 113) identifies, within every child, the 'fundamental human urge to be effective, competent and independent'. Echoing this belief, Carr's learning story approach (2001) foregrounds the strands of the *Te Whāriki* (New Zealand Ministry of Education, 1996) curriculum of well-being, belonging, contribution, communication and exploration as a frame for observation of a child. Wardle and Vesty have discussed how practitioner reflection on documentation of children's dispositions to learning and their attitudes and approaches within the provision supports their well-being and resilience. The positive lens of the learning story provides a picture of the child that can be meaningfully and genuinely shared with children and with parents in partnership.

Claxton and Carr (2004) propose that, by observing *how* children learn, we focus on the dispositions and attributes of their learning, and, consequently, our support in this context is in developing the 'robustness, breadth and richness' of their learning. Podmore *et al.* (2001) drew on the learning story dispositions to formulate the child's perspective through a child's questions for each of the dispositions: 'do you know me? can I trust you? do you let me fly? do you hear me? is this place fair for us?' (ibid.: 8). Just as Laevers advocates use of his observation scales as a tool to evaluate provision, so the articulation of the child's perspective through the questions encourages practitioners to scrutinise their practice and pedagogy.

More recently, Carr (2011) has collaborated with teachers in a number of New Zealand early childhood centres to extend the purposes of the learning story, beyond a record of children's learning, into an active tool in supporting their learning through a dialogic review. In the centres in the small-scale project, the children, families and teachers contribute to the stories, which remain constantly and readily accessible. Children, families and practitioners engage with them dynamically, engaging in episodes of sustained shared reflection on the story that supports the child in reviewing their learning and following their interests, while allowing the adults to monitor their learning.

Similarly, the preschools of Reggio Emilia regard documentation of children's learning to be a central and active part of early childhood teaching and learning. Observation of, and dialogue with, children contribute to the picture of the child's learning to create a 'concrete and visible memory of what they said and learn in order to serve as a jumping-off point for next steps in learning' (Edwards *et al.*, 1998: 10). Dahlberg *et al.* (2007: 147) propose that the process of pedagogical documentation itself is a 'social construction ... where pedagogues, through what they select as valuable to document are also participative co-constructors'.

Documentation can take the form of photographs, examples of work at different stages of completion or written and video recordings of children's interactions, and it has an equally prominent place in the displays of the setting as the finished products. The act of displaying the *process* as well as the *product*, the *how* as well as the *what*, in itself conveys a strong message of the importance of the characteristics of the child's effective learning. Like the positive lenses of Laevers' scales and Carr's learning stories, the documentation of the Reggio Emilia preschools and infant–toddler centres positions children as 'active participants in the organisation of their identities, abilities and autonomy . . . and each individual child, with inborn abilities and potential that are extraordinarily rich, powerful and creative' (Malaguzzi, 1992, in Scott, 1996: 39).

Interestingly, and in a similar vein, MacDonald's study (2012) gave children cameras to record their experiences of mathematical measurement within their lives outside the setting. Allowing the child control through the possession of the camera elicited the child's perspective on their learning and understanding, with some surprising results. The dialogue between researcher and child around the photographs enabled the researchers to gain insight into the children's creative and divergent mathematical concept formation.

These forms of observation require us to join the child in dialogue and as co-constructors, to be receptive, responsive and respectful. If we regard learning as a social process, then we observe the child within a social context, in play and interactions with peers and adults, as well as alone. These observations can be immediate and spontaneous, as well as sustained and planned, and can include the child's voice and views on their own learning.

This model of observation allow us to demonstrate our knowledge, understanding and valuing of the individual child's uniqueness – watching children's *doing* reveals a rich seam for discovery of their processes and agendas for learning, eminently suitable for sharing with parents to include their contributions, as they inform us of their child's fascinations, interests and learning in the home.

These approaches to observation and assessment inform practitioners for planning of more than activities and next steps up the developmental ladder. They enable planning for possibility thinking (Craft *et al.*, 2007) through environments, experiences, relationships, interactions and encounters in learning, where children are seen as 'confident explorers, meaning-makers and decision-makers' (ibid.: 10). They require Epstein's (2007: 1) 'intentional teacher', who uses her 'knowledge, judgment, and expertise to organise learning experiences for children; when an unexpected situation arises (as it always does), they can recognise a teaching opportunity and are able to take advantage of it, too'.

It is surely to be welcomed that theoretical perspectives on children's learning and internationally renowned practices in observing that learning can be seen to inform English guidance for best early years practice in the EYFS requirement to report on characteristics of effective learning, which is currently in place as this book is being written. Lesley's encounter below demonstrates how some settings are embracing this opportunity with enthusiasm, motivated by the possibility of developing their practice in a new direction.

Encounter: turning assessment upside down

Lesley is an early years professional leading practice in a private nursery. She is proud of the provision and of the staff. Priorities within the organisation are that the children have as much access as possible to interesting and varied outdoor provision, and that staff move from room to room with the children as they grow older, maintaining the bonds formed between key person, child and family and providing familiarity and support at transition. Lesley has identified how that practice has, at times, been challenging for individual staff members, but celebrates the fact that it has provided opportunities for personal and professional development within her team of 'girls'. She speaks of them warmly, 'This group of girls we have working here now, they're the best yet'.

Practitioners in the nursery provide parents with a written report on children's progress once a term, supplementing their ongoing learning journeys. The mother of one of the children in the nursery is a foundation stage teacher in a nearby school and she has shared with Lesley how the foundation unit is approaching reporting on children's characteristics of effective learning to parents. Lesley is fired with enthusiasm as she describes it to me and how she feels it will match so well to the ethos of her setting:

> What we would do is provide every parent with information on the topics we have covered in the room that term, and the adult outcomes that were planned in each area of learning and development. All parents get the same information about what the children have been taught about, and the learning journeys tell them about their child's individual progress (and they will probably know all that anyway, because we will have talked about it together as it happens, more or less on a daily basis with most of our families). But what the girls spend their time writing their reports about is how the child is learning. And these girls know that – they know their children inside out. So we turn the whole thing upside down, and the focus for us all, children, parents, practitioners, changes from what to how.

This further encounter, from a local authority adviser, reiterates the extent to which effective practitioners know their children.

Encounter: moderator's reflection

During the local authority moderation process of this year's (2013) EYFSP, it was evident just how well many of the teachers knew their children. The moderation process involved discussions about children against the profile statements and levels; the moderators purposefully asked open questions, such as, 'Tell me about James', to encourage the teachers to talk. As they talked, they were able to provide examples of work, anecdotes, photographs, written observations and snippets of conversations they had had with children and their families; often, these did not have a physical piece of evidence to go alongside, but the teachers' warmth and enthusiasm as they spoke about children left the moderator in no doubt that they really knew their children and could make sound, informed professional judgements against the profile statements. Mostly, the physical evidence was extensive, and some examples of very creative record keeping using technology were evident: moderators were shown interactive slide shows, voice recordings, videos and video books that all added to the picture of that child. At the end of the meeting, moderators often felt like they knew the children the teachers had discussed so well.

This encounter evidences how practitioners, in this case reception teachers, draw on their shared experiences with children to provide what Geertz (1973) calls 'thick description', in order to interpret the children's complex learning within the setting and community in a way that proves eminently meaningful for the moderator.

In the autumn of 2013, the first statistical data of results for the EYFSP was released (Department for Education, 2013). The release states that 52 per cent of children in England achieved a good level of development, defined as, 'achieving at least the expected level within the three prime areas of learning: communication and language, physical development and personal, social and emotional development and the early learning goals within the literacy and mathematics areas of learning'.

This statistically stark figure is further broken down to inform that, whereas 60 per cent of girls achieve this good level of development, only 44 per cent of boys do so. The release uses the terminology of a competition, of scores and goals in relation to the seventeen areas of learning and development. For those many children who are not able to achieve this outcomes-led goal, a child-led form of assessment, such as a report on the child's characteristics of effective learning, may present a more positive addition to the picture of the child.

Before the first EYFSP statistics were released, however, the Department for Education had launched and closed a consultation based on proposals to reduce the status of the EYFSP from statutory to non-statutory. In its place is proposed a 'simple check' (Thornton, 2013) to be performed at the beginning of reception, with proposals that a range of tests be made available by providers for schools to choose and administer, and that, if adopted, data from the check would replace EYFSP data. If adopted, these proposals may further pare down the information gathered about a child's development, reducing it to those aspects that can be checked, and again removing consideration of their ways of learning from the statutory requirements of good practice.

Transition to Key Stage 1 or 2

For some children, transition from early years provision to statutory schooling is accompanied by a stark change in pedagogical approaches.

Encounters: at transition

At transition meetings at the receiving school, Anne always supplemented her paper records with a verbal 'picture' of the children's individual learning journey through their time in nursery. She was particularly pleased to be able to describe Jasmina's progress from an initially hesitant and cautious beginner, dependent on adult support to access the provision, to a confident explorer, clear in her choices and deeply engaged in and prepared to take on challenges in her preferred learning experiences, especially with peers. She was thoroughly dismayed to see the receiving teacher write one word next to Jasmina's name – 'lazy'.

And, for another teacher: Jenni is a new teacher in the school, leading the foundation unit team. Soon after her appointment, she meets the Key Stage 1 teacher to discuss transition arrangements. The head of primary also attends the meeting. Jenni discusses the observations and assessments she has been accustomed to completing to inform her knowledge of and planning for the children. She uses her observations to inform the opinion she delivers of each child's learning and development and their developing dispositions and attitudes to learning. The head of primary breaks into her discussion.

> We don't do observations in school. We use the children's work. We assess that, and that tells us all about the child's learning. If there is any problem, we see a dip in their standards and can put in some extra help.

The foundation stage teachers in these encounters had been accustomed to a form of assessment that celebrates the unique child's learning processes; however, for some teachers, particularly those of older children, paper-based assessment of skills, knowledge and understanding may be where their experience lies (Walsh *et al.*, 2010), and they may be challenged by a more individual, open-ended form of assessment. Fisher (2011: 40) proposes that this is especially true of recently trained teachers (within the last 10 years), and, additionally, that the value and purpose of observation may need to be explained to colleagues and senior staff, who may otherwise perceive that teacher to be 'doing nothing'. The challenge can be compounded by a lower adult-to-child ratio in older classes, increased requirements and expectations of the school and of the curriculum (and, hence, of the child), as well other internal and external pressures.

This discontinuity of approach experienced by practitioners and children between the stages can also be experienced by parents at transition. For them, from now on, an exchange of information about their child's learning and development may take place on a termly basis, rather than their accustomed daily, or at least regular, basis (Shields, 2009). Additionally, the form of assessment can change from an individual picture of their unique child to a set of data or scores against standardised tests. With only 52 per cent of children assessed as achieving the expected good level of development in the EYFSP (Department for Education, 2013), such reports may be a disheartening experience for many parents of young children who are just beginning their statutory schooling. The key role that parents play in their children's learning, recognised so powerfully in the findings of the Effective Provision of Pre-School Education (EPPE) Project (Sylva *et al.*, 2004), continues beyond the foundation stage, as is recognised by good practice in many schools. In these cases, a triangulated sharing of knowledge between the child, the setting and the home allows continuity of learning, acknowledging the complementary importance of each social context for the child (Bronfenbrenner 1979).

Research can indicate, however, that many small-scale studies have addressed some of the barriers to adopting an active approach to learning in schools and can report some positive findings. Roberts-Holmes' study with head teachers (2012: 40) discovered a recognition of the appropriateness of the EYFS approach to children's learning and development within the early years of statutory schooling and a concern, not for achieving school-readiness, but rather for 'making the school ready for the child'. He also discusses their perception of the tension between the principle of the competent unique child and assessment against predetermined standards at the end of EYFS, citing Anning (2009, in Roberts-Holmes, 2012: 36) who defines it as a 'direct conflict'.

Walsh *et al.*'s study (2010: 63) in Northern Ireland of a limited introduction of an 'Enriched Curriculum . . . of play based and age appropriate curriculum for four- to six- year-old children' reports a smoother transition into schooling, and child observations indicated improved dispositions to learning. Walsh also discovered that teachers of the older children were challenged by observational assessment practices, more accustomed as they were to the more traditional, paper-based assessment methods.

Martlew *et al.*'s study (2011: 74) with class teachers trying to introduce an approach that they define as 'active learning' identifies the tension between the more outcomes-led assessment processes of the classroom and the less formal processes of early years assessment. Without the typical written evidence provided by 'children's work' to capture children's learning, some of the teachers in Martlew's study turned to journals, big books and learning stories.

The Pen Green project, Making Children's Learning Visible (Hayward and McKinnon, 2014), evidences a complex, interrelated, pedagogical approach to supporting children's development within early years settings and schools. The initial step involves staff in drawing up their 'image of the child', negotiating their values for the children in the setting and how they want them to be (ibid.: 70).

The Pen Green Centre image includes 'confident and strong, able to question . . . to choose . . . to assert themselves, to be empathetic, to be secure' (ibid.: 70). Discussion then identifies those children who may be vulnerable and so need additional or different support. Video footage of children, and children in interaction with practitioners, is used to support practitioners to reflect on how well their pedagogy supports the 'image' and the individual child. Assessment of the child against EYFS early learning goals is completed through dialogue with practitioner and family. Each discussion and step in the process draws on the sustained and detailed documentation that informs knowledge of the individual child. The project reports how successfully this model of visible learning was used to support pedagogical dialogue at transition into school and across stages and year groups within participating primary schools.

Each of these studies indicates a willingness and intention to retain the child at the heart of provision within some schools and brings with it implications for reception and Key Stage 1 classes to provide similarly enabling environments, physical and emotional, and possibilities for effective learning as those experienced by children in the early years of their care and education.

Provocations

- Do you, as an individual and as a team, approach children's learning with 'wide eyes and open minds'? What more could you do to ensure you observe what is happening, rather than what you planned to see?

- Is there a different model of observation that you could add to your repertoire to allow you to see a little more of the picture of the child?

- Who is involved in discussion of children's ways of learning and developing in your setting? Are the child's and family's voices reflected well?

- Does your observed knowledge of children's interests, preoccupations, dispositions and ways of learning inform your provision?

References

Athey, C. (1990) *Extending Thought in Young Children: A Parent–Teacher Partnership*. London: Paul Chapman.

Blenkin, G. and Kelly, A. (eds) (1992) *Assessment in Early Childhood Education*. London: Paul Chapman.

Bronfenbrenner, U. (1979) *The Ecology of Human Development*. Cambridge, MA: Harvard University Press.

Brown, V. (2013) The possibilities for assessment. In Woods, A. (ed.) *Child-Initiated Play and Learning: Planning for Possibilities in the Early Years*. London: Routledge.

Carr, M. (2001) *Assessment in Early Childhood Settings: Learning Stories*. London: Paul Chapman.

Carr, M. (2011) Young children reflecting on their learning: teachers' conversation strategies. *Early Years: An International Research Journal* 31(3): 257–70.

Claxton, G. and Carr, M. (2004) A framework for teaching learning: the dynamics of disposition. *Early Years: An International Research Journal* 24(1): 87–97.

Craft, A., Cremin, T., Burnard, P. and Chappell, K. (2007) Developing creative learning through possibility thinking with children aged 3–7. In Craft, A., Cremin, T. and Burnard, P. (eds) *Creative Learning 3–11 and How We Document It*. London: Trentham.

Dahlberg, G., Moss, P. and Pence, A. (2007) *Beyond Quality in Early Childhood Education and Care: Languages of Evaluation*, 2nd edn. Abingdon, UK: Routledge.

Department for Education (2013) *Statistical First Release*. Available online at: www.gov.uk/government/uploads/system/uploads/attachment_data/file/252223/SFR43_2013_Text.pdf (accessed 27 October 2013).

Donaldson, M. (2006) *Children's Minds*, 2nd edn. London: Harper Perennial.

Drummond, M.J. (1993) *Assessing Children's Learning*. London: David Fulton.

Edwards, C.P., Gandini, L. and Forman, G. (1998) Introduction: background and starting points. In Edwards, C.P., Gandini, L. and Forman, G. (eds) *The Hundred Languages of Children: The Reggio Emilia Approach to Early Childhood Education*, 2nd edn. Greenwich, CT: Ablex, pp. 5–25.

Epstein, A.S. (2007) *The Intentional Teacher: Choosing the Best Strategies for Young Children's Learning*. Washington, DC: National Association for the Education of Young Children.

Fisher, J. (2011) Building on the Early Years Foundation Stage: developing good practice for transition into Key Stage 1. *Early Years: An International Research Journal* 31(1): 31–42.

Geertz, C. (1973) *The Interpretation of Cultures: Selected Essays*. New York: Basic Books.

Gopnik, A., Meltzoff, A. and Kuhl, P. (1999) *How Babies Think*. London: Weidenfeld & Nicholson.

Hayward, K. and McKinnon, E. (2014) Making children's learning visible: uncovering the curriculum in the child. In McKinnon, E. (ed.) *Using Evidence for Advocacy and Resistance in Early Years Services: Exploring the Pen Green Research Approach*. Abingdon, UK: Routledge, pp. 68–85).

Karlsdóttir, K. and Garðarsdóttir, B. (2010) Exploring children's learning stories as an assessment method for research and practice. *Early Years: An International Research Journal* 30(3): 255–66.

Katz, L. (1993) *Dispositions as Educational Goals: ERIC Digest*. ERIC Clearinghouse on Elementary and Early Childhood Education, Urbana IL. Available online at: http://files.eric.ed.gov/fulltext/ED363454.pdf (accessed 17 July 2013).

Laevers, F. (ed.) (2005) *Well-Being and Involvement in Care Settings: A Process-Oriented Self-Evaluation*. Leuven: Kind & Gezin and Research Centre for Experiential Education. Available online at: www.kindengezin.be/img/sics-ziko-manual.pdf (accessed 20 September 2012).

MacDonald, A. (2012) Young children's photographs of measurement in the home. *Early Years: An International Research Journal* 32(1): 71–85.

Malaguzzi, L. (1992) *A Charter of Rights*. Reggio Emilia, Italy: Municipality of Reggio Emilia.

Malaguzzi, L. (1998) History, ideas, and basic philosophy: An interview with Lella Gandini. In Edwards, C., Gandini, L. and Forman, G. (eds) *The Hundred Languages of Children: The Reggio Emilia Approach – Advanced Reflections*, 2nd edn. Greenwich, CT: Ablex, pp. 49–97.

Martlew, J., Stephen, C. and Ellis, J. (2011) Play in the primary school classroom? The experience of teachers supporting children's learning through a new pedagogy. *Early Years: An International Research Journal* 31(1): 71–83.

New Zealand Ministry of Education (1996) *Te Whāriki*. Wellington, NZ: Learning Media.

Nutbrown, C. (1996) Wide eyes and open minds: observing, assessing and respecting children's early achievements. In Nutbrown, C. (ed) *Respectful Educators – Capable Learners: Children's Rights and Early Education*. London: Paul Chapman.

Nutbrown, C. (1999) *Threads of Thinking: Young Children Learning and the Role of Early Education*, 2nd edn. London: Paul Chapman.

Podmore, V., May, H. and Carr, M. (2001) The 'child's questions': programme evaluation with *Te Whāriki* using 'teaching stories'. *Early Childhood Folio* 5: 6–9.

Powell, S. and Goouch, K. (2012) *What in the World is Happening to Babies? A Critical Perspective of Research and Support for Baby Room Practitioners in England*, paper presented at TACTYC Annual Conference. Available online at: www.tactyc.org.uk/pdfs/Reflections-Powell-Goouch. pdf (accessed 24 September 2013).

Roberts-Holmes, G. (2012) 'It's the bread and butter of our practice': experiencing the Early Years Foundation Stage. *International Journal of Early Years Education* 20(1): 30–42.

Rogoff, B. (2003) *The Cultural Nature of Human Development*. New York: Open University Press.

Scott, W. (1996) Choices in learning. In Nutbrown, C. (ed.) *Respectful Educators – Capable Learners: Children's Rights and Early Education*. London: Paul Chapman.

Shields, P. (2009) 'School doesn't feel as much of a partnership': parents' perceptions of their children's transition from nursery school to reception class. *Early Years: An International Research Journal* 29(3): 237–48.

Sylva, K., Melhuish, E., Sammons, P., Siraj-Blatchford, I., Taggart, B. and Elliot, K. (2004) *Effective Provision of Pre-School Education (EPPE) Project: Final Report*. Nottingham, UK: DfES.

Thornton, L. (2013) *Changes to Early Years Assessment Proposed: Consultation into Primary Assessment and Accountability Could Introduce New 'Baseline Check'*. Available online at: www. optimus-education.com/changes-early-years-assessment-proposed-consultation-primary-assessment-and-accountability-could#sthash.QqPaoWHg.dpuf (accessed 27 November 2013).

Vygotsky, L.S. (1978) *Mind in Society*. Cambridge, MA: Harvard University Press.

Walsh, G.M., McGuinness, C., Sproule, L. and Trew, K. (2010) Implementing a play based and developmentally appropriate curriculum in Northern Ireland primary schools: what lessons have we learned? *Early Years: An International Research Journal* 30(1): 53–66.

Wood, D.J., Bruner, J.S. and Ross, G. (1976) The role of tutoring in problem solving. *Journal of Child Psychiatry and Psychology* 17(2): 89–100.

Index